50 STRATEGIES for Motivating Reluctant Readers

Heidi Crumrine

Consultant

Heather Keller, M.Ed.

Publishing Credits

Corinne Burton, M.A.Ed., *President* and *Publisher*
Aubrie Nielsen, M.S.Ed., *EVP of Content Development*
Kyra Ostendorf, M.Ed., *Publisher, professional books*
Véronique Bos, *VP of Creative*
Cathy Hernandez, *Senior Content Manager*
Kevin Pham, *Graphic Designer*

Image Credits

Photographs on page 32 by Heidi Crumrine and Lisa Godwin. All others Shutterstock.

A division of Teacher Created Materials
5482 Argosy Avenue
Huntington Beach, CA 92649
www.tcmpub.com/shell-education
ISBN 979-8-8855-4340-8
© 2024 Shell Educational Publishing, Inc.
Printed in USA BRP001

Table of Contents

Introduction

Strategies

Appendices

Welcome

Learning to read did not come easily to me. This might seem like a strange thing to admit at the beginning of a book about literacy instruction, but the experience has informed my teaching and of course this book. I know what it means to struggle, and I know what it means to be a student who is trying to learn. I grew up in a house surrounded by books, read to by parents and grandparents, and showered with love and support. I had the best of circumstances. And yet, I struggled.

I spent all of first grade seeing the words on the page and understanding them, but then being unable to explain the text to my teachers. I would read the words out loud and be redirected, but I didn't understand why. Turns out, due to chronic ear infections, I had developed a 50 percent hearing loss and couldn't convey to my teachers what I was reading inside my head. I spent all of first and second grade going to "the reading van" and getting extra help. I hated it. I knew that none of my friends needed this, and I was endlessly frustrated because in my mind, reading made sense.

Finally, in third grade, my teacher pulled me aside to tell me that I was being moved up to the grade-level reading group. I was thrilled. I finally felt seen. As an adult reflecting back on this experience, I have a lot to consider. I now realize that, of course, I deserved to be in a group where I saw myself. I deserved to feel heard by my teachers. I deserved to feel as though I was a reader, not a reluctant reader. I didn't see myself as reluctant, struggling, or at-risk, but I am sure that my teachers saw me that way. Luckily, they never articulated that to me. They kept teaching and encouraging me and eventually I got to where I wanted to be.

The rest of elementary and middle school were relatively uneventful for me. I read. I wrote. I got good grades. But I didn't love what I was doing. I didn't feel the passion I felt the summer after third grade when I first read Laura Ingalls Wilder's *Little House on the Prairie*, got to page 100, and realized how far I had come. Reading in school had become a task, not a passion, a job without a purpose. I see much of this in the work of my students as well. The joy of school and love of learning gets lost somewhere in middle school along with a mess of hormones and puberty. It wasn't until I was home on college break that I found myself starting to read again for pleasure. Once I was back in the habit of reading, I never stopped. When I realized that reading was learning and learning could come from my own interests, I wished I had learned that sooner. As a teacher, my primary goal is to ignite or reignite that spark in my students sooner than it happened for me.

This is a book written by a teacher for teachers. Each of the strategies or activities suggested here can be used for literacy instruction. And many work wonderfully in any content area to support students' reading skills. It is my hope that after reading this book you will feel empowered to try something different to engage and connect with your students in new ways!

I would be remiss not to thank those in my life who helped me in putting this book together. Good teaching is about collaboration with others, and I am very lucky to have some of the best who inspire me to be better every day. I sought out each of these educators for their expertise in their particular area because I knew that no one would know better. For that, I thank you!

- Jane Newton, reading and English language learner teacher, Concord High School: Jane, we were hired the same year at CHS and have been connected ever since. You've taught me everything that matters about reading instruction and your fingerprints are all over this book.

- Amanda Neidhart, third-grade teacher, Broken Ground Elementary School: Amanda, you welcomed my baby into your third-grade class, and in the process, welcomed me too. She was new to the school, and it is because of you that she has blossomed at BGS and will continue to blossom wherever she goes.

- Sam Neil, my Teacher of the Year sister and Space Camp roommate from Kansas: Thank you for your brilliant ideas, for your passion for public education, and for sharing with me TikToks late at night.

And to my mom, Dr. Edie Perkins, the best middle school reading and language arts teacher I've ever known. So much of my inspiration and success as an educator comes from a lifetime of watching you work magic in the classroom, motivating countless students to love reading!

—Heidi Crumrine

Reading as an Essential Skill

I must judge for myself, but how can I judge, how can any man judge, unless his mind has been opened and enlarged by reading.

—John Adams, reflecting on the rights of people to choose their rulers (1761)

There is a wonderful and tangible joy that emanates from a young child who has finally learned to read. A whole world has opened up to them. They are excited, they are devouring books, and they are proud of themselves. As a parent I have watched this transformation happen with my own children and as a teacher I have watched it happen in my classroom. Learning to read is a special milestone; watching a child learn to love reading is even more special.

The value of strong literacy skills for all students is not just about their performance in school. It is not about their test scores, and it is not about what (often seemingly arbitrary) reading level they are on. It is not about phonics, or structured literacy, or spelling tests, or i-Ready, STAAR, or NAEP testing. It is about their futures. When our students leave our classrooms with strong literacy skills, they are set up to succeed on whatever paths they choose to travel in life.

It is not a stretch to suggest that effective literacy instruction is an act of equity. If students aren't making progress with literacy skills, regardless of their age, they are being set up for failure as adults. This is a sobering reality. There are any number of reasons why a student might struggle with literacy skills, but there are a limited number of outcomes for those students who do.

When students struggle with literacy skills, it is not just about the mechanics of reading. They face an uphill struggle to succeed in their content-area classes, and, as they age up in school, no longer is language arts the only challenging subject for students with weak literacy skills. Not surprisingly, students who struggle with academics across the board report feeling marginalized, left behind, and confused (Learned 2018). They are at a greater risk of dropping out of high school, which then leads to a host of other roadblocks in their ability to launch into adulthood.

In addition to students struggling with the *how* of reading, there is also the issue of students struggling with the *why* of reading. A growing problem among students is aliteracy. Aliteracy is the result of the skill of reading having been acquired, but not the will. In other words, students can read, but they choose not to. According to a recent report, 46 percent of children surveyed ages 6 to 8 reported reading for fun five to seven days a week, and yet only 18 percent of 12- to 17-year-olds reported the same (Scholastic 2022). The report indicates that the number of students who enjoy reading decreased from 2010 to 2022. Adolescents today are not reading enough, and it is having a direct impact on their literacy skills.

As educators, we should have a laser-like focus on literacy equity. We want our students to be literate and thoughtful members of our global society. It can be frustrating to see students who are disengaged or seemingly disinterested in reading, but we have many tools in our toolbox available to help them. Our students might appear frustrated, but that doesn't mean we as teachers have to be.

Sparking a Passion for Reading

Recently, while I was checking out at a local big-box store, my cashier was a former student. He had been a student in an English credit recovery course I taught a few years before. He liked coming to school but he didn't like doing school. He had failed nearly every course his freshman year because he didn't complete any work. He came to school nearly every day and sat through nearly every class but didn't do a thing on his own. He would participate in class, engage with his teachers, and participate in group work, but he just couldn't follow through outside of the classroom.

However, he loved to read. He devoured books. He especially loved dystopia, fantasy, zombies, and vampires. I couldn't keep up with his habits and by the end of the year he had read close to 30 books. The last time I saw him was on the last day of school. He almost bumped into me because his nose was buried in a book as he walked out of school. The final book in his favorite series had been released earlier that week and he had been telling me about it for weeks. "I got it!" he told me with a grin as he held up the book with pride.

When he handed me my receipt, he said to me, "I hope you're doing well, Mrs. Crumrine. Whenever I see a book, I think of you."

This exchange reminds me why I love what I do and also why I believe in what I do. At the core of my approach is a calculated and deliberate focus on giving students time and space to read books that they choose, that they are passionate about, and that are at their level. This is unarguably one of the most important components of my reading program, and it is not because it's quiet in the classroom and students are "just reading," as some of my colleagues suggest as they walk by my room. They're quickly gifted with an earful about the value and benefit of independent reading, and they often then comment, "I wish my English teacher had done that."

My efforts to ignite or reignite in my students a passion for reading are what bring me the most joy in my job. I am genuine and humble in my desire to encourage other teachers to consider a similar approach. I take to heart the words of Kelly Gallagher in his book *Readicide*: "Our highest priority is to raise students who become lifelong readers. What our students read in school is important; what they read the rest of their lives is more important" (2007, 117). To spark a love of reading in a young person is to set in motion a pathway for success that will follow them wherever they go. We don't need to be the gatekeepers; we give our students the gift of books, and they can open any door that stands before them.

Practices for Promoting Reading

The goal of this book is not to wade into the waters of how to teach the mechanics of reading, but, rather, to provide strategies to engage any reader regardless of instructional model. Students struggle for many reasons, and this is not a book about a specific intervention or instructional approach that is tied to a specific philosophical or pedagogical bucket. Regardless of *how* you teach reading, each of these strategies can be integrated into your classroom in ways that support, motivate, and even inspire students to find joy in reading.

Help Students Find the Right Texts

When I first started teaching, students who were not engaged with and seemingly did not enjoy reading were labeled as "resistant readers." Over time, that label evolved to "reluctant readers," perhaps because of a less negative connotation. Students who struggle with or are disengaged with reading are not necessarily resistant to it, but they might be reluctant because of how hard it can be for them. I struggle with the label "reluctant reader" because I believe that reluctance is related to circumstances. Anyone will be motivated by the right circumstances. All too often when I sit with a student who announces that *I don't read*, they will follow that up with a kind of story or type of reading that they do enjoy.

I firmly believe that deep down, everyone loves to read. Those who say otherwise just haven't found the right book yet. So, what can we do about this? As a classroom teacher, I have modified my approach to reading instruction in a way that shifts my teaching away from a one-size-fits-all method to a balance between using whole-class texts and offering students choice. If we want our students to become better readers, then we need to give them opportunities to do that. They need to read books at their level and books that interest them. They need to have time in class to read and time in class to talk about books. Real readers, I tell my students, read. And they don't answer multiple-choice questions after each chapter every time they do it.

Say Yes to Students' Interests

I cannot begin to tell you how many conversations I have had with friends and colleagues that center around the content of the books their students or children are reading. "But he only reads *Diary of a Wimpy Kid*!" they will say to me. "So?" I reply. "He's reading!" All too often, as educators (and parents), we try to create experiences for our students that match the ones we had as young people. You might say, "But I loved *Pride and Prejudice* when I was in high school!" Yes, you did love that book, but it doesn't mean that your students need to love it too.

I'm also willing to bet that before you found your way to *Pride and Prejudice*, you devoured a lot of other books first that brought you joy and that made your parents shake their heads. This doesn't mean that you should never have any say in what your students read, and it doesn't mean that they should always read whatever they want. What it does mean is that you should seek to find something that they love as much as you loved *Pride and Prejudice*, and that inspires them to keep reading and thinking about the world around them. It's not about the book. It's about the experience; it's about the skills they grow while reading; it's about seeing themselves reflected in a book as they seek to better understand the world and their place in it.

The notion of offering students choice in their reading is not just something that is fun or in the vein of "everyone wins a trophy." It is supported by research in the area of motivation and literacy. There is a strong correlation between students' interest in a particular topic and the likelihood that they are engaged in reading about that topic (Neugebauer 2017). Similarly, research indicates that choice is particularly useful for engaging reluctant readers (Allred and Cena 2020), and that students having a voice in what they read leads to positive associations with reading and their language arts classes (Cantrell et al. 2017). According to the previously mentioned Scholastic report (2022), across all demographics, 93 percent of kids name their favorite books as those that they choose themselves, and 92 percent of students say that when they pick out a book for themselves, they are more likely to finish it.

Which brings me to *Captain Underpants* and *Doctor Proctor's Fart Powder*. If that's what they're reading and they're happy, then be happy for them and share in their joy. Once you have them hooked, you can begin to guide them toward other stories beyond those they normally read. If they like funny books, there are many other funny books out there beyond what may typically be given to them. Follow their lead and let them surprise you.

This is all to say that when we find a variety of ways for students to be engaged with their reading, help them feel a sense of ownership over their learning, and strive to make connections, we are setting our students up for success, regardless of their circumstances.

Give Room for Lots of Reading

I provide a lot of independent reading time during which students are allowed to choose texts at both their level of interest and their reading level. Choice can then serve as an extrinsic motivator, which increases the likelihood the student will be engaged and interested in reading. Research suggests that the use of independent reading as an extrinsically motivating instructional technique can be an effective way to increase student engagement in their language arts classes (Allred and Cena 2020; Gilson, Beach, and Cleaver 2018; Tegmark et al. 2022).

In general, the correlation between independent reading and the improvement of specific literacy skills such as fluency and vocabulary growth is hard to tease out. However, there is research that correlates reading volume with improved literacy outcomes, particularly fluency (Allington and McGill-Franzen 2021; Erbeli and Rice 2021; Wilhelm and Smith 2016). Earlier research supports this same correlation. Hasselbring and Goin (2004) found that the number of books read and the amount of time spent reading were most strongly correlated with reading comprehension ability.

This data matches what is referred to as *the Matthew effect*, theorized by Stanovich (1986). This effect suggests that a student who reads well will have a larger vocabulary, struggle less with reading, and thus be motivated and capable of reading more. Reading more will result in an increase in literacy skills and thus motivate the student to read still more, and so on. Conversely, a student who struggles to read will have a less robust vocabulary, become frustrated and disengage with reading, read less, and thus not grow their literacy skills.

This makes a strong case for increasing the volume of what students are reading. Since teachers cannot control what kind of texts or how much their students are reading outside of school, it makes logical sense to use independent reading in the classroom to increase this volume, and thus increase fluency and other comprehension skills necessary for reading success.

Assess Thoughtfully

Many of the strategies in this book are designed to extend a particular skill you are teaching in your classroom. In these instances, student work doesn't always need to be assessed, but if you decide to do so, consider a few important points:

Make sure that your purpose in assessment is clear. Are you assessing reading or writing?

- If you are assessing reading, and a student produces writing that is weak but indicates a strong understanding of the text, then your feedback needs to center on reading skills and not writing.

Similarly, if you are a content-area teacher and you have assigned a text to your class, what is your goal?

- Is the goal to assess reading comprehension of a grade-level text? Or is it to introduce them to content?
- If the goal is to introduce students to content, is that text accessible to all students? Is a student disengaged or struggling because they can't read it? That means they can't access your content, which means they need a more accessible text to learn the content.

Clarifying assessment goals can sometimes be challenging for teachers, but if our goals in assessment are clearly articulated from the beginning, then it will be easier to provide meaningful feedback for students.

Culturally Responsive Teaching and Learning

Culturally and linguistically responsive teaching expert Sharroky Hollie defines a culturally responsive mindset in the following way: "Being culturally responsive is an approach to living life in a way that practices the validation and affirmation of different cultures for the purposes of moving beyond race and moving below the superficial focus on culture" (n.d.-a, para. 2). When educators use culturally responsive teaching strategies, students are more engaged, which in turn helps them to be more successful academically.

VABB with Your Students

As Hollie states, culturally responsive teaching helps students understand "when to use the most appropriate cultural and linguistic behaviors for any situation without losing who they are culturally and linguistically" (n.d.-b, para. 4). This happens when educators Validate, Affirm, Build, and Bridge within their learning environments. When you validate students' home environments, you legitimize their home cultures and languages. Affirmation works to end the negative stereotypes associated with non-mainstream cultures. Once this initial work has been started, build deeper relationships with students by showing them that you care and understand their home cultures. Finally, give students the skills they need for success by showing them the bridges to mainstream culture.

What is VABB?

Validate

Affirm

Build

Bridge

Provide a Print-Rich Environment

Culturally and linguistically responsive classrooms are print-rich and display the linguistic supports all your students, especially multilingual learners, need to be successful. This includes the academic vocabulary that students are learning, which they need to access to be able to discuss language and content. In addition, these classrooms are active. Students are engaged in discussions with peers and teachers. They physically move around the room to work with peers on a variety of projects. The materials being utilized reflect a variety of cultures and perspectives, and student work is prominently displayed and honored.

Culturally and linguistically responsive educators use texts with characters and pictures that represent their students. They encourage students to research areas of interest and produce art that validates and exhibits their cultures. Culturally and linguistically responsive educators are constantly reevaluating their curricular choices to ensure all students are represented and validated.

Taking a culturally and linguistically responsive stance is a holistic approach. It embraces the whole learner. When students feel they belong, are validated, and are represented in the curriculum, they are open and connected to the learning. Teaching in this manner allows for everyone's story to be told.

How to Use This Book

Choose a strategy and give it a try! Some strategies include student activity pages, which are provided in Appendix C as well as digitally. (See page 87 for more information about the Digital Resources.)

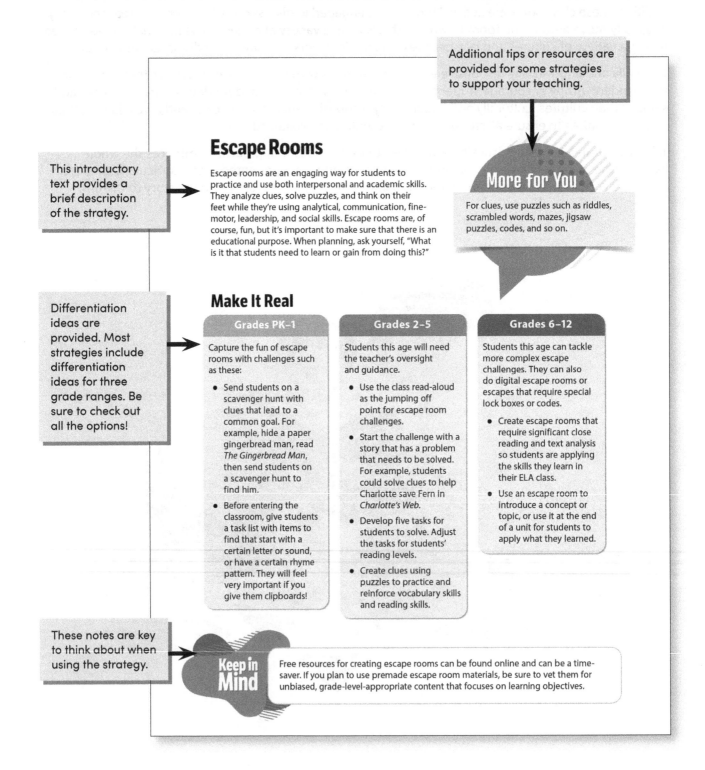

This introductory text provides a brief description of the strategy.

Differentiation ideas are provided. Most strategies include differentiation ideas for three grade ranges. Be sure to check out all the options!

These notes are key to think about when using the strategy.

Additional tips or resources are provided for some strategies to support your teaching.

Escape Rooms

Escape rooms are an engaging way for students to practice and use both interpersonal and academic skills. They analyze clues, solve puzzles, and think on their feet while they're using analytical, communication, fine-motor, leadership, and social skills. Escape rooms are, of course, fun, but it's important to make sure that there is an educational purpose. When planning, ask yourself, "What is it that students need to learn or gain from doing this?"

More for You

For clues, use puzzles such as riddles, scrambled words, mazes, jigsaw puzzles, codes, and so on.

Make It Real

Grades PK–1	Grades 2–5	Grades 6–12
Capture the fun of escape rooms with challenges such as these: • Send students on a scavenger hunt with clues that lead to a common goal. For example, hide a paper gingerbread man, read *The Gingerbread Man*, then send students on a scavenger hunt to find him. • Before entering the classroom, give students a task list with items to find that start with a certain letter or sound, or have a certain rhyme pattern. They will feel very important if you give them clipboards!	Students this age will need the teacher's oversight and guidance. • Use the class read-aloud as the jumping off point for escape room challenges. • Start the challenge with a story that has a problem that needs to be solved. For example, students could solve clues to help Charlotte save Fern in *Charlotte's Web*. • Develop five tasks for students to solve. Adjust the tasks for students' reading levels. • Create clues using puzzles to practice and reinforce vocabulary skills and reading skills.	Students this age can tackle more complex escape challenges. They can also do digital escape rooms or escapes that require special lock boxes or codes. • Create escape rooms that require significant close reading and text analysis so students are applying the skills they learn in their ELA class. • Use an escape room to introduce a concept or topic, or use it at the end of a unit for students to apply what they learned.

Keep in Mind

Free resources for creating escape rooms can be found online and can be a time-saver. If you plan to use premade escape room materials, be sure to vet them for unbiased, grade-level-appropriate content that focuses on learning objectives.

Structures and Routines

Structures and routines support learning by helping students focus and attend to the task at hand. When students know what to expect, they feel safe, and as a result, they feel more connected and are thus more willing to take risks. Establishing routines is also efficient for the teacher. If we have certain touchstone experiences or situations in our classrooms, we can build around them. The strategies in this chapter work as literacy routines for any grade level. Like all routines, they take some time to become established and familiar, but in the long run, they support literacy instruction and students' diverse skill levels. If our goal is to create a community of readers, then it's important to have routines that make reading a positive and engaging experience at various points and in various ways throughout the day, month, and year.

The Strategies

The Classroom Library

A classroom library full of texts from a variety of genres and unique voices and at different reading levels offers students much more than just access to books. It offers them choice and agency in the books they engage with while providing a visual representation of the idea that literacy is at the core of all that we do in school. In addition, providing a well-stocked classroom library is an act of equity that ensures a book-rich environment for all students. The goal is to generate excitement and expose students to different kinds of books.

Make It Real

Grades PK–1

- Make sure books are at children's eye level and hand level. Organization can be by topic of interest. Use bins to house the books.

- Encourage students to choose books on their own.

- Create topical displays of books combined with realia to support content currently being studied in the classroom.

- Display books that have been read aloud in a special location so children can easily find and read them.

Grades 2–5

- Organization can move away from reading level and toward genre. When students browse the library, they can focus on area of interest.

- Teach students how to choose books. They can look at the title and cover, read the first page or two, look for authors they have read before, and so on.

- Since the purpose of the classroom library is to provide a low-stakes way for kids to explore a variety of texts, it's okay if they're choosing books above or below their reading levels.

Grades 6–12

- Organization can be by genre; concept; subject; recommendations by students, parents, or teachers; and so on.

- Students this age often gravitate toward ideas more than genres. Examples include Strong Women, Dragons, Witches and Wizards, Death and Dying, and Stories of Survival.

- For reluctant readers, the classroom library is a tool for the teacher to connect with the student. When others have settled into a book, the teacher can grab several off the shelf and recommend choices in a low-stakes, personalized manner.

The Classroom Library *(cont.)*

Keep in Mind

- Making a classroom library visually engaging is an important part of accessibility for all students. Using Canva, you can create labels, signs, and descriptions that are engaging and informative. Consider asking your students what would appeal to them or how they would like the library organized.

- Provide books that represent your students and their interests, backgrounds, and stories. In addition, include perspectives and voices of those who are not typically represented in your classroom.

- Curating a classroom library does not have to be expensive or overwhelming. Look for books at used bookstores, thrift shops, flea markets, and so on. Invite parents to donate books their children no longer need.

- If you don't have your own classroom, collaborating with the media specialist can be a lifesaver. The specialist could keep a cart of books in the library that is reserved for your students to browse when they go to the library.

Book Talks

A book talk is a brief promotion for a book, designed to increase exposure to a text and encourage students to read it. Like a commercial or a public service announcement, the purpose is to provide a large group the information that might hook them to read the book. An effective book talk includes a brief summary and a read-aloud of an engaging passage. Added bonuses are watching a book trailer (created by the publisher or found on YouTube), looking at images from a film version, or hearing from other students who have read the book.

Book talks don't need to be solely the responsibility of the teacher. As community is built in the classroom, students can be encouraged and are often excited to do their own book talks. They can be formal (as an assessment) or informal (as a daily routine). Parents can be invited to record book talks for their favorite books. Other teachers and administrators could also be guest book talkers, as well as former students!

Make It Real

Grades PK–1	Grades 2–5	Grades 6–12
• Give book talks for a few read-aloud options and allow the class to choose the book you read. • As students' literacy skills grow, they can share books with a small group or the whole class. • Students can bring favorite books from home to share. • Along with picture books and story books, include informational books in your book talks.	• Presenting book talks regularly from the beginning of the year helps foster a sense of community of readers. • Give book talks that support content learning. During a unit on the American Revolution, for example, talks could include books on that topic.	• Student book talks don't need to take long (fewer than five minutes) and can help to establish and nurture a community of readers. • Showcase books that are above and below student reading levels. All students should see books that are achievable for them in book talks.

Keep in Mind

- Using technology for book talks increases accessibility for students who struggle with public speaking, have IEP or 504 accommodations, or are not able to attend school. A tool like Flip (formerly Flipgrid) allows students to create and post content on a class website. Other students can view classmates' book talks and respond.

- Use books in the classroom library, but also give book talks on titles that are popular with students, newly published, or connected to another content area.

- Represent multiple perspectives in book talk choices. Students need to be able to see themselves and also see others who are different from them in the books being shared.

First Chapter Friday

First Chapter Friday (FCF) is a classroom routine during which the teacher reads out loud the first chapter of a book every Friday (or whatever day they choose). Use FCF to provide exposure to a variety of texts, perspectives, and voices that students may not encounter on their own and to encourage them to make connections across content areas or to connect books around a common theme or narrative thread. Guests (the principal, other teachers, former students, and parents) can also be invited to share the first chapters from their favorite books!

Make It Real

Grades PK–1

- Rather than FCF, you may wish to adopt the routine of "First Page Friday." Select a book from the library and read one or two pages to pique students' interest.
- After reading the first page, have students make predictions about the story. Place the book in the classroom library for students to read on their own.

Grades 2–5

- For this age, FCF can begin to include an actual first chapter of a book.
- Adjust the number of pages you read based on the attention span of your students. As students grow, you can read more, but it's important to remember that FCF is a sneak peek only, and if students struggle to pay attention, it defeats the purpose.

Grades 6–12

- Secondary teachers often want to read books aloud but struggle with finding time to do so. FCF is a great way to infuse reading aloud into the classroom and curriculum.
- Incorporate student choice by asking students what kinds of stories they like, and choose books to feature accordingly. You can then expand students' horizons from there.

Keep in Mind

- First Chapter Friday is a more in-depth peek into a book than a book talk and can be a natural follow-on from a book talk. Or, after a few book talks, have students vote on which book's first chapter they would most like to hear.

- Engage students in choosing books. They can nominate books or bring in books from home.

- Students' interest tends to wane after about ten minutes of read-aloud. That might mean you abridge the chapter, which is okay.

- FCF should be about community building, offering students exposure to a variety of texts and voices and letting students enjoy listening to a book. Avoid asking students to complete FCF worksheets—this dampens students' enjoyment of hearing books read aloud.

What's My Teacher Reading?

It is important for students to see their teachers as part of the classroom reading community. If teachers are going to ask students to read widely and talk about what they're reading, then teachers need to do the same. For this reason, I share what I am reading with my students. I find it is beneficial to use some kind of visual—a chart, pictures of book covers, a reserved spot on the board—that I add to and then casually refer back to in conversations. This is a powerful way to show students that I am living the reality I ask of them.

Make It Real

Grades PK–1	Grades 2–5	Grades 6–12
• Share images of books you read and loved as a child. • Share a book you read to your child or gave as a gift, or a new title you are considering for the classroom library. • Share informational books such as how-to books, cookbooks, gardening books, travel books, magazines, and so on.	• The books you share will need to be creatively targeted to students' ages. Include some of your favorite books from when you were this age. • Share informational books such as nonfiction texts you are reading, historical books, and so on, summarizing the content as appropriate for your students.	• Display a chart that you add to as you finish books. It can be displayed for students to see but does not need to be a central part of your daily routine. • Add to the chart while students are reading their independent reading books. This gets students' attention but doesn't take away from instructional time.

Keep in Mind

When students learn that teachers read outside of school, they see modeling that they may or may not see at home. Keep in mind that students don't need to hear about *every* book you are reading. In some instances, sharing about a book you are reading could introduce topics that may not be appropriate for the level of your students.

My Favorite Page

My Favorite Page isn't so much a routine as it is a way to build community around books and extend any of the routines presented previously. It can range from a reflective activity to a meaningful assessment that capitalizes on student choice and creativity. The directions are simple: Students select their favorite page from a book they have read and then photocopy it and mark it up. You can set a purpose for their work based on literacy objectives, or students can annotate freely. If having every student photocopy a page is a challenge, consider these work-arounds:

More for You

See page 82 for Tips for BookSnaps (grades 5–12).

- Each week, choose one student to create their favorite page. Arrange with the media specialist for the student to go to the library to photocopy the page.
- Have students working in small groups agree on one page to duplicate and annotate.
- Have each student choose their favorite quote, illustrate it, and explain their choice.

Make It Real

Grades PK–1	Grades 2–5	Grades 6–12
• Provide several different photocopied pages at a learning center. Ask students to choose the one they like best and respond to prompts such as: "Color words you recognize in blue; color all the vowel teams in green; draw an illustration you think is missing from this page."	• For a picture book, have students identify a favorite page and add thought bubbles or speech bubbles for the characters. • For a chapter book, have students illustrate a favorite paragraph, adding thought bubbles or speech bubbles for the characters. • Have each student share their page with a classmate, and explain why it is their favorite.	• Students can highlight a favorite line, annotate the page, complete low-key literary analysis, add symbols as illustration, or make connections to other texts, world events, or personal memories. • Students can create BookSnaps, harnessing the popularity of apps to react, add stickers, filters, and so on.

Keep in Mind

- Model how you select a favorite page and think aloud as you annotate, highlight, and so on. Ask students: What makes something memorable in a story?
- Students can use Google Slides, PowerPoint, or Canva, and add stickers, emojis, GIFs, or even music. Have students share their work on the class or school website.
- Have students share their work with another teacher, student, or administrator. Or they could share with an adult or mentor in their lives.

Student Choice and Agency

Choice is a powerful motivator for students in any classroom and at any age. Motivation is complex and influenced by intrinsic factors as well as societal, familial, and environmental factors. A lack of motivation in the classroom is problematic because it affects academic performance. Jung-Sook Lee found a correlation between motivation and performance, noting that "students with higher levels of emotional engagement showed higher levels of behavior engagement and this led to higher reading scores" (2013, 182). Intrinsic motivation is the single most powerful factor in determining behavior, and the stronger a student's intrinsic motivation, the better the student's learning behaviors (Tokan and Imakulata 2019). Tapping into students' passions supports their intrinsic motivation and has the potential to positively impact their academic skill development. When we offer students choice and a sense of agency in their learning, we are doing just that.

The Strategies

Independent Reading

Independent reading is an essential element of a classroom that values student choice and meets students where they are in terms of their interests and skills. Independent reading refers to time during class when students self-select their reading. This most often happens during the literacy block or in the ELA classroom. How teachers utilize the time varies, but at its core is the notion that students choose their own books and are given time during class to read them. Providing time in class for independent reading ensures that all students—including those who don't read at home—spend time reading texts they have chosen.

Make It Real

Grades PK–1	Grades 2–5	Grades 6–12
• Provide wordless picture books to engage pre-readers. • Have students choose books that interest them and use the time to explore the books, paging through them and reading them as they are able. • Start with short amounts of time, about five minutes, building up during the year as students' reading skills and attention spans grow. Use a timer.	• Independent reading can be an offshoot of instructional reading time. All students should have an independent reading book on hand. • When the teacher is working with one group of students, and the other students have completed their assigned work, they can read their self-selected books. • Establish a consistent time each day for independent reading to ensure that all students have time to read. After lunch is a popular time for this.	• Though it can be challenging in secondary classrooms, some reading time is better than none. That can mean, for example, eight minutes a day in a 45-minute period, or longer time periods twice a week. • Students can apply concepts taught during instruction (literary analysis, etc.) to their independent reading texts. Applying what they have learned to self-selected books at their own level gives students greater access to content and supports their learning.

Keep in Mind

- Ideally, students are reading books at their independent level. However, if a student is highly motivated and engaged by a particular book above or below their level, they shouldn't be held back. I've seen many students devour books that are above their level.

- If you are going to offer choice, then you will need to say "yes" to a variety of texts. That makes books like *Captain Underpants* not only okay but encouraged.

- Older students may wish to read non-traditional digital texts such as fan fiction or text-based games. In the vein of saying "yes," if your situation supports this, it can be an excellent way to hook students.

Book Clubs

During a book club, students talk with their classmates about a chosen text and make sense of it together while growing their comprehension skills. Teachers provide varying levels of support depending on the needs of the students, but the goal of a book club is ultimately for students to discuss the book and share their perspectives—what they liked or disliked, their thoughts about the characters, ideas about the theme, and so on. Book clubs serve several purposes: they nurture a love of reading, they support discussion of texts, they nurture reflection, and they can help develop student independence. Hold book clubs periodically, such as once a week.

Make It Real

Grades PK–1

- Book clubs work best with small groups. The teacher facilitates the book club discussion while the other students are engaged in independent tasks such as center work.
- The teacher helps students agree upon a book to be read.
- Depending on students' reading skills, the teacher can read the book aloud, students can choral-read, or they can do a combination of these.

Grades 2–5

- Book clubs can be based on students' current instructional reading groups or other groupings.
- Offer a selection of books for students to choose from.
- Facilitate the book club discussion by preparing questions in advance.
- As students gain skills, they can be coached to lead the book club discussions.

Grades 6–12

- Provide text sets around common topics from which students can choose. For example, you could offer a text set related to the theme of justice/injustice.
- Provide instructional support related to the theme and then encourage students to apply what they learned during the book club.
- Have students use the Book, Head, Heart protocol (page 45) to support the discussion.

Keep in Mind

- Book clubs don't need to be limited to fiction. Students can choose a nonfiction topic of interest and read articles or texts from sources such as TIME for Kids (timeforkids.com) and the Smithsonian (si.edu/kids). There are informational texts available at nearly every reading level, and many are free and can be accessed online.

- I find that older students tend to be more focused when we are working on a common skill that they then apply in their book club. For example, if we are learning about symbolism, I provide instruction about what it is, share examples from a common text, and then give focused directions for students to practice during their book club meetings.

- Assistive technology such as Read&Write and NaturalReader may be used to support students as needed to read grade-level texts.

Book Tastings

A book tasting gives students the chance to sample a variety of books before choosing one to read. Similar to a cake tasting for a wedding, you give students a sample of what's available by setting out books for them to "taste." Put placemats on tables and set books on the placemats. Arrange the tables by topics, themes, genres, and so on—whatever is appropriate for the level of your students. Set a specific goal that you articulate to students to keep them engaged and focused!

More for You

See page 83 for My Book Tasting Notes (grades 3–12).

Make It Real

Grades PK–2	Grades 3–12
• Offer a modified version of book tastings using musical chairs. Place books on chairs and play music. When the music stops, children sit in the closest chair and explore the book. • Facilitate book tastings for small groups of students while the other students are completing independent tasks such as center work. • Give students a goal for choosing a book: choose one to take home, choose one to read during independent reading time, and so on.	• A combination of chapter books and rich picture books can be offered for students in these grades. • Provide note-catchers for students to capture their impressions of books and indicate ones they want to read. Note-catchers can include space for students to record the title, author, genre, impressions of a book, and whether they are interested in reading it. • Use book tastings to introduce students to books to choose from for book clubs.

Keep in Mind

- Students do not need to spend more than three to five minutes with one particular book. The idea is to allow students to explore many titles.

- If you wish to be extra-creative, make the book tasting like a tea party. Find lace doilies at a dollar store, and serve juice, herbal tea, or hot cocoa in teacups. Set up placemats and books and invite students to wear fancy hats. As an alternative, feel free to simply place some books on tables and set the kids loose. Both options can work!

Flip Your Story

When students read a text, instead of asking them to retell or summarize, have them flip the method of storytelling. Students can think about the text from a different character's perspective or turn a text into a series of graphic-novel-style frames, a movie trailer, or a children's story. There are many possibilities, but the point is for students to be given different options to manipulate what they learned to create a new version.

Make It Real

Grades PK–1

- Begin with a questioning routine. For example, for *The Three Bears*, ask questions such as these and have students draw their ideas:

  "How would baby bear tell this story?"

  "What did the bear family do while they were away?"

  "Draw the bear family's outing."

- Have students illustrate the story using the "Somebody, Wanted, But, So" format.

Grades 2–5

- Use a whole-class read-aloud as the foundation for students to show what they know.

- Have students create a picture book version for younger children. Partner with a lower-grade class, and have students read their books to the younger students.

- Students can turn the book into a board game: What piece represents each character, what is the goal, and what are the barriers?

- Have students write a letter or thank-you note from one character to another character.

Grades 6–12

Options for students to flip the story include:

- Create a soundtrack for the text by making a playlist.

- Turn the story into a graphic novel.

- Write a "missing" chapter from the book.

- Write one or more diary entries from the perspective of the main character.

- Create a podcast where students talk about the big ideas.

- Make an infographic that conveys the big ideas of the book.

Keep in Mind

Allowing students the opportunity to decide how they communicate their understanding of a text (or anything, really) gives them both agency and voice in their work. Sometimes they know better than we do, and when we give them the opportunity to show us, they gain both engagement and confidence in ways that we could never create for them.

Show Me What You Know

In early February one year, my normally lively and boisterous students were coming to class with a look of resignation and a feeling of blah. I realized that they were coming to school like adults sometimes go to work. They were going through the motions, feeling they had little voice in what we were going to do. I decided they needed a voice in what and how they learned.

Which brings me to a strategy that caused me anxiety but led to excellent outcomes in student work: allowing students to decide how to show what they know. This strategy works particularly well when students haven't had a choice in what they read. Students can choose options such as those in the Flip Your Story strategy (page 26), or they can show their knowledge in other ways. The point is to put them in the driver's seat and empower them to show what they know, not what they think we think they should know.

Make It Real

Grades PK–1

When meeting with small groups, plant the seeds for thinking differently about a story by asking questions such as these:

- "How could you draw what you know?"
- "How could you act out what you know?"
- "What could you build to show what you know?"
- "What could you create to show what you know?"

After the discussion, give students time to choose and complete an activity to show what they know.

Grades 2–5

Give students options with a focus:

- "Do you want to show how your character has grown up by making a high/low chart or by drawing before and after pictures?"
- "Could you show me the most important moments in the story by making a time line?"
- "How can you show me the three parts in this story that you liked the most?"

Grades 6–12

Pick a competency and let students choose how they show proficiency. Use questions such as the following to prompt their thinking:

- "What is the best method for showing the message of your story?"
- "How can you create something that evokes the same emotion as your book?"
- "What do you want to say about what's going on in your head?"

Keep in Mind

- When assessing students' work, ensure that the focus is on the reading skill, not the product.
- Giving choice doesn't have to mean unlimited, completely open-ended choices. Choice within a selection of options is still offering choice.
- Ask students for their ideas! Tell them the goals of the assessment (what you are looking for) and then ask them to brainstorm suggestions.

Collaboration and Community

Building a community in the classroom and school is arguably the most important part of creating a space where learners are engaged and excited to learn. Learning can be messy and challenging, and all students will have moments of struggle and frustration, but if there is a foundation of trust, those moments will feel less scary, and students will be more willing to persist. The following strategies support community-building—in the classroom, in the school, and with the wider community—and can happen at any time during the year.

The Strategies

50 Strategies for Motivating Reluctant Readers—136022

© Shell Education

Book Buddies

Book buddies pair a younger and an older student, with the purpose of forming a connection and practicing reading skills. Typically, each older student selects a book and then reads to their younger buddy. Sometimes the younger students are doing the reading; at other times the older students are doing the reading. Students enjoy the social component—younger children get attention from older ones, and older children get to be positive role models. In addition, older students gain a sense of pride in nurturing younger learners. The only downside with creating these connections is that you will wish you could do it for every child in every school.

Make It Real

Grades PK–1	Grades 2–5	Grades 6–12
• Pre-readers will benefit from being read to by their older buddies. You may wish to have these students select the books they would like their older book buddies to read to them. • Emergent readers can read out loud to their older book buddies. Encourage them to practice reading their books before the buddy session to build fluency and confidence.	• These students might have a younger book buddy or an older one. Both instances provide a perfect opportunity for students to practice reading out loud, which builds their fluency and confidence. • Students at these levels can read picture books or portions of chapter books with their book buddies. Adapt as needed based on the students.	• Consider the personality and needs of the older students so they're well-matched to support the younger students. • Plan for some sessions during which students share their favorite books with their younger buddies. • Coach students to ask their book buddies questions about the text and discuss it during and after reading.

Keep in Mind

- Work with a teacher at a lower or higher grade level to develop a book buddy program. Determine how students will be paired up and when you'll meet.

- Plan for 30-minute sessions once or twice a month in a multipurpose room or the library.

- Prior to each session, help students select the books they are going to read and practice reading them aloud to build fluency.

Read-Aloud

Read-aloud is exactly what it sounds like: You read a text, often a book, aloud to your class. It can be tied to your curriculum, but it can also be unrelated to content. Children of all ages love to be read to and not everyone has that kind of experience at home. Reading aloud models fluency and prosody, making the listening experience enjoyable and helping to create a community of readers. In addition, reading aloud fosters students' interest in books, supports understanding of story conventions, and develops listening comprehension and vocabulary.

Make It Real

Grades PK–1	Grades 2–5	Grades 6–12
• Read-aloud should be part of the daily routine for young students. • Reading aloud culturally diverse books will help children see themselves in texts and make connections to the experiences of others. • Reading aloud can serve as a good transition between activities and is a good way to settle and refocus students after recess, lunch, or P.E.	• Children in these grades love to hear both picture books and chapter books. • Providing choices in what will be read aloud helps students feel a sense of ownership. • Read-alouds can be above the independent reading levels of students. Students can comprehend at higher levels than they can read, and reading aloud can expose striving readers to engaging and compelling texts.	• Reading aloud is often less common due to class schedules, but it is worth the effort. • Read-aloud options include full long-form texts, chapters of shared texts, short stories, poetry, and picture books. • Don't underestimate the power of a good picture book for older readers!

Keep in Mind

Reading aloud is an effective way to introduce and reinforce a range of literacy skills:

- Model predicting, inferring, and making connections while reading.
- Stop periodically and ask students to share their insights, questions, or predictions.
- Connect the read-aloud to what students are learning in another content area.
- Have students use a response journal to reflect on the text.

Avoid giving assignments related to a read-aloud. You really can "just" read to your students. We all know it's more than just reading.

March Bracket Challenge

Take advantage of the energy of college basketball playoffs by creating a bracket challenge for books, poems, characters, illustrators, quotes, or themes. Create brackets with 16 titles and then have students read or study each one and vote to determine the top 8, then the final 4, and then have a championship round to determine a winner. Harness students' excitement around competition and watch their engagement skyrocket. Of all the things I've done, I have never seen my students more engaged than when we embed a bracket challenge into our work together. I always do it during March, but that's not a requirement!

Make It Real

Grades PK–1

- Students can determine their favorite fairy tale, illustrator, or picture book.

- Read two books each day, and have students vote on their favorite. Continue until the final brackets have a winner.

- Have students write opinions about which book is their favorite and why. They then vote again.

Grades 2–5

- Students can vote on their favorite read-aloud, the character they find most inspiring, or the book that they think every student their age should read.

- This lends itself well to a cross-curricular unit. Students can make bar graphs during math, engage in dramatic activities such as reader's theater, and so on.

Grades 6–12

- Focus on texts that all students have access to. Poetry works well for this.

- One approach is to spend 15 minutes at the start of class on a poem. After all the poems have been covered, students vote, and then revote, to get to the top two.

- Have students work in small groups to choose one of the top two to dig into and analyze more deeply. The goal is to become experts on the piece and advocate for it.

Keep in Mind

- Have students hone argument skills through writing or discussion as they debate and vote on their choices.

- Bracket challenges are a fantastic way to infuse skill reinforcement. While reading a poem with older readers, for example, you could analyze literary techniques; consider theme or message, notice patterns, or make connections between or among the brackets.

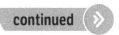
continued »

March Bracket Challenge (cont.)

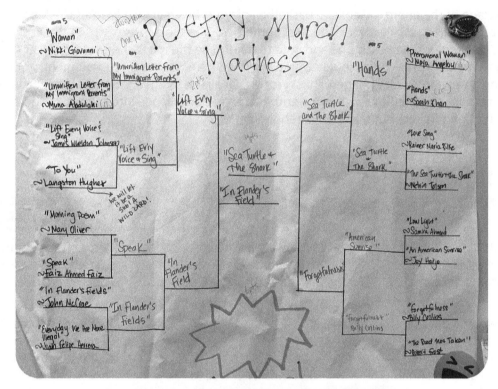

Partner with Other Adults

You don't need to be the only one fostering a reading community. Inviting parents, other adults at the school, and members of the community to come read to and connect with students is powerful for community building. Most adults are thrilled to be invited as guests. The visitor can choose a story to read, or they can read a chapter or selection from a class text. You can establish a schedule, for example inviting a guest once a month, or you can invite guests as opportunities arise.

Make It Real

Grades PK–1	Grades 2–5	Grades 6–12
• Invite parents or caregivers to be guest readers. If they can also share a family tradition, even better. • Invite the principal, an administrative assistant, a custodian, or another teacher to be a guest reader. • A student's birthday is a good opportunity for them to invite a guest reader to class to read their favorite story.	• Ask students to help identify possible guests. Students might suggest staff from the local after-school club, scouting organization, and so on. • Consider inviting community members such as music teachers, veterinarians, medical professionals, small business owners, and so on.	• Invite parents, other adults in the building, or community members to join a discussion about a text. Give the adults the text ahead of time. • Consider asking students to invite a former favorite teacher to come and participate in the discussion.

Keep in Mind

- Set up a guest appearance using a video conferencing tool such as Zoom, or have a guest record a reading using a video-based tool such as Flip (formerly Flipgrid). Students can then record a response to be shared back with the guest.

- Don't hesitate to reach out to authors, local celebrities, and so on. Many are more than happy to visit via video conference if they can't come in person.

- Have students take ownership of the process. They can collaborate as a class to decide whom to invite and then to write the invitation.

All-School Reading Challenges

Reading challenges harness the power of friendly competition to motivate students to read to reach a particular goal together. Students can be challenged to read a specific number of minutes, pages, or books; collectively read a variety of genres; and so on. The goal is not to pit students against one another but rather to celebrate reading progress and highlight the success of individual classes and the school community as a whole.

More for You

Reading Bingo (grades PK–2)—see page 84.

Reading Bingo (grades 3–5)—see page 85.

Make It Real

Grades PK–1

- Create a Bingo card for students to complete. Include tasks such as read outside, read a book with a friend, read a book out loud to a stuffed animal, listen to someone read to you, and so on.

- Provide time for students to complete the reading challenges at school to ensure everyone has an equitable way to participate and contribute to the class goals.

Grades 2–5

- Create a series of reading challenges that students can check off at their own pace. For example, read a new author, read a book that has pictures, read a book recommended by a classmate, and read a book that won an award.

- This approach allows students to select texts that interest them while meeting a goal and being celebrated for it.

Grades 6–12

- Create challenges that engage the larger community without pitting individual classes against one another. Consider school challenges such as staff vs. students, the humanities department vs. the STEAM department, and the east building vs. the west building.

Keep in Mind

- Pitting students or individual classes against one another in a binary win/lose scenario can exacerbate feelings of incompetence in struggling readers. Set up the challenge to celebrate the success of the group rather than focusing on specific individuals.

- Students can compete against themselves by setting a goal based on their interests and needs and then celebrating meeting that goal whenever it happens.

Integrating Drama

Drama instruction is often viewed as play, as something that can happen when the "real" instruction has been completed. However, drama is a powerful and motivating strategy to use for literacy instruction. Integrating drama and reading has multiple benefits—it increases engagement and motivation, increases personal connections to literature, deepens thinking, and helps students explore the perspectives of others (Bogard and Donovan 2022). Connecting drama and reading is a natural combination as "drama was the first way in which humans shared their history, myths, and stories" (Erickson 2016, para. 1). Each of the following strategies puts drama at the center as a tool for engagement. You don't need to teach theater to incorporate elements of the theater in your classroom!

The Strategies

Act Out a Passage

Instead of asking students questions about what happened in a text and why it happened, task students with acting it out. They don't need to write or create a script. This can be done collaboratively as a whole class, in groups, or individually. Students will need to dive deeply into a text to find important details and make meaning from the text. Acting out texts also helps students in the audience better comprehend them through watching the performances.

Make It Real

Grades PK–1

- Have students act out an important scene in a story. They can take on roles or make puppets to use.

- Support students in acting out the scene by coaching them and asking questions. For example, help students think about how the characters are feeling: "How do the other mice feel when Frederick shares his poem? How can you show that with your face and body?"

Grades 2–5

- Ask the class, "What are the main events in this story?" Make a list together and then assign events to different small groups of students to act out.

- Have each group work collaboratively to create their scene. Then have the groups perform their scenes in succession to tell the story.

- Students don't need to read from the text while performing—they can use words or phrases that are the most important.

Grades 6–12

Have students act out a scene with various challenges:

- Give students a word bank and require students to use those words in their scene.

- While a group is at the front of the class, the rest of the class tells the group what scene to act out.

- Have each group create a different ending to the story and act it out.

Keep in Mind

- The purpose is to help students understand big ideas, characters, and events of a story.

- Students who are shy or reluctant to take a role in a scene can collaborate with the group to make props or write a short script.

Tableau

Tableau comes from a French phrase referring to a scene or story presented by motionless figures. In other words, a "freeze frame." To create a tableau from a text, students must work together to determine how to effectively represent what matters from the text. After students have read a text, have them work in pairs or small groups. Ask them to think about how their bodies will be placed, what their facial expressions will be showing, what they will be "doing," and so on. Give students time to practice the scene; then have them present their frozen scenes to the class.

Make It Real

Grades PK–1	Grades 2–5	Grades 6–12
• Have students start by creating a frozen image showing an emotion from the text, such as love or surprise. You can also ask them to show different actions, such as running, and "freeze." • Read a text together and then, as the whole group, create an important moment from the text.	• Use a common text as the foundation for the tableau, but have students work in groups. Give each group a different scene from the text. • Give students a purpose for their tableau so they have a focus as they create their freeze frame.	• Have students create a tableau that represents a concept, for example, justice in *To Kill a Mockingbird*, or the message of an op-ed the class read together. • Each group of students can present several tableau scenes in succession in slideshow style.

Keep in Mind

- Select from a variety of texts for a tableau—informational texts, poetry, or film in addition to fiction texts.

- When students are presenting, count down "3-2-1, freeze!"

- As students are presenting a tableau, have the rest of the class guess the scene being portrayed.

- Extend the tableau by allowing the group to incorporate one movement into their scene.

Charades

Charades engages students in acting out characters and scenes from a text without using words. To prepare, students need to think about the character or event and consider how to effectively communicate it to others using only body movements, gestures, and facial expressions. Everyone is engaged because they are either presenting or guessing. Charades can be a powerful tool for helping students take on the perspectives of others through role-play. It also helps build problem-solving and collaboration skills.

Make It Real

Grades PK–1	Grades 2–5	Grades 6–12
• Choose characters from a nursery rhyme or story and talk with students about the traits of a character. Then have students act out the traits. • Whisper a character's name to a student and have the student act out the role while the other children guess who it is. • Have small groups act out scenes from a book.	• Have students act out a character or situation from a text, act out a new word or concept, or act out a theme or message. • Provide vocabulary words and have students act them out. Write the words on strips of paper and allow a student to draw one and then act it out while the other students guess the word.	• After students have read part or all of a text, identify themes in it (love, justice, injustice, etc.). Assign small groups of students to different passages or chapters and give them the task of creating a scene from the text that conveys one of the themes; then have the other students guess the theme.

Keep in Mind

- It's important to have a focus when using charades to support reading to ensure that it has an educational purpose.
- Purposeful charades can focus on a common text or theme, or charades can be used as a tool for a student to show understanding and complexity of thought.

Character Interviews

Flip the idea of bringing in a person to interview and instead invite students to interview the character/s in a text. Doing this is engaging for students and both demonstrates their understanding of the text and supports thinking more deeply about it. Begin by having students complete K-W-L charts for the character. This helps students analyze what they know about a character and think about what they would like to know. Then have students develop questions they would like to ask the character. Below are suggestions to spark your own thinking about how to inspire students to both interview and then respond to questions about what they are reading!

Make It Real

Grades PK–1	Grades 2–5	Grades 6–12
Work with students as they develop questions to ask a character. Questions for Sylvester from *Sylvester and the Magic Pebble*: • How did you feel when you found the magic pebble? • What lesson did you learn about how to use the pebble? • What will you do next now that you are a donkey again? • What other things would you like to wish for?	Prompts for *Charlotte's Web*: • Ask students to imagine they are newspaper reporters interviewing Fern after the state fair. What would they ask? How would Fern reply to the questions? • Tell students Fern has become a spokesperson for People for the Ethical Treatment of Animals (PETA). What is her platform?	Examples for *Romeo and Juliet*: • Provide students with a list of sample questions that dig into a character's likes, dislikes, motivations, and so on. Students can use these as models to craft questions to ask Romeo. • If Romeo were a guest on Oprah, what would she ask him and how would he respond? • If Romeo were brought into the police station to be questioned about Tybalt's death, what would he say?

Keep in Mind

- After students have developed questions, have them answer the questions. This could be done by simulating a news interview or a talk show interview, by having students write the responses, or by discussing the responses as a whole class or in small groups.

- If you simulate an interview with the character, students can take on varying roles: interviewer, interview subject, or audience member.

Improv

Improvisation invites students to assume the persona of a character and make in-the-moment decisions about how the character would act in a particular scenario. Students use the text to learn about the character and their emotions and responses to situations. They then use the information from the text to enact how the character might react in a different situation. An important rule of improv is "Yes, and . . .", which refers to the idea that an improviser builds on whatever another improviser has said or done. Improv supports student engagement and encourages creativity, collaboration, and teamwork.

Make It Real

Grades PK–1	Grades 2–5	Grades 6–12
The teacher can "be" the character, and students can tell the teacher how to act.	As students get older, they can begin to move from concrete scenarios to ones that require making inferences.	These students can think beyond a text and use knowledge of a character to create new, but realistic, situations.
Examples for *Sylvester and the Magic Pebble:*	Example for *Charlotte's Web:*	Example for *Romeo and Juliet:*
• Sylvester takes the pebble home. What does he say to his parents about it? • Sylvester takes the pebble to school and the other students want to hold it. What does Sylvester do?	• Fern tells Charlotte her biggest secret—how do they both act? • Fern tries to sneak Wilbur into school—what does she do?	• Juliet has to run errands for her mom and tries to swing by Romeo's castle to catch a glimpse of him. • Lady Montague goes to get her nails done and trash talks Lady Capulet to the nail tech.

Keep in Mind

- For younger students, create concrete or text-based scenarios.
- For older students, the scenarios can be more inferential. The teacher can create the scenarios, or, if appropriate, the students can do it.
- Asking a question with the scenario helps focus students of any age and is particularly helpful with younger students.

Reading Comprehension

Reading comprehension refers to understanding what we read. It is the product of word recognition, language comprehension, and other bridging processes including fluency, vocabulary knowledge, and morphological awareness (Scarborough 2001; Duke and Cartwright 2021). Proficient readers are strategic, intentionally using higher-order thinking processes to make meaning of what they are reading (Shanahan 2018). The following strategies are engaging and require students to use higher-order skills to think more deeply about and show their understanding of texts. These strategies are also collaborative in nature, which means that students can learn from one another regardless of individual reading levels.

The Strategies

Hot Seat

The idea of hot seat is that students play the role of a character from a text and answer questions posed by classmates (Wilhelm 2013). The purpose is for both the student in the hot seat and the students questioning the character to be engaged in higher-order thinking about a text. Hot seat supports students in exploring characters' motivations and developing such skills as making inferences, developing questions, and summarizing.

Make It Real

Grades PK–1

- The teacher can take the hot seat to answer questions.

- After reading a text, work with students to develop questions to ask the character. Questions can focus on the character's daily life, actions, motivations, and so on.

- Informational texts can also be used; in this case, the teacher takes on the role of an expert, such as a scientist.

Grades 2–5

- Work with students in small groups and have them select the characters they will role-play and prepare for questions.

- Provide direct instruction to students about how to ask questions. Have all students prepare questions for the characters.

- Teach students how to ask questions that go beyond simple factual answers to questions that require deeper levels of thinking about the text.

Grades 6–12

- Groupings can vary—students can work in pairs taking turns as the role-player and the questioner, a panel could answer questions, or single students can answer questions.

- Students asking questions can take on a role from a perspective in the book, or they could be an outsider from the text entirely, such as a journalist.

Keep in Mind

- Prepare students for both roles—the character and the audience asking the questions. The character needs to be prepared to authentically answer in their role, and the audience needs to be prepared to craft questions that match the character and the tone/purpose of the text.

- Introduce hot seat as a warm-up activity at the beginning of class. Take the hot seat and let students ask about your weekend, your favorite book, or your favorite foods. Students who are comfortable could also take the hot seat. Invite another adult in the building to join the warm-up hot seat in your classroom!

STEAM Challenges

Combining literacy and STEAM challenges gives students an opportunity to demonstrate their learning with hands-on projects. Students are highly engaged and also work on collaboration and communication skills while engaged in these challenges, which is a win no matter what their product looks like.

Make It Real

Grades PK–1	Grades 2–5	Grades 6–12
Examples include:	Examples include:	Examples include:
• Design a new wing of Cinderella's castle to include rooms for her beloved animals. • Read *Owen & Mzee: The True Story of a Remarkable Friendship* and then design a shelter for them to live in together outside. • Read *The Snowy Day* and build a quinzhee (snow shelter) outside.	• Build the boat that Max travels on in *Where the Wild Things Are*. • Use Legos® to build Fern's barn from *Charlotte's Web*. • Create a piece of art that represents a message or theme from *Indian No More*.	• Redesign Camp Green Lake from *Holes* so that the residents get the support and skills they need. • Research and then create a windmill after reading *The Boy Who Harnessed the Wind* and learning about renewable energy. • Using design software, design the dream house for the Lee family from *A Raisin in the Sun* (or use Legos!).

Keep in Mind

- Support connections between literature and the sciences by having students read a fictional text or poetry and a related informational text prior to giving the STEAM challenge. Possible topics include farms, bees, robots, hibernation, trees, weather, flight, stars, ponds, and more.

- STEAM challenges don't need to be overly specific in terms of product. Give students a variety of materials and have them create from there. In a Literature of Survival class for high schoolers, I provided straws, pipe cleaners, tongue depressors, paper, and cardboard and told them to design a structure that would withstand a windstorm. I used a classroom fan placed at varying distances to determine a winner.

What's Going On in This Picture?

"What's Going On in This Picture?" is a popular weekly column offered by the New York Times Learning Network during the school year. Each week, the column presents an intriguing photograph with no caption or context. Teachers share the photo with their students and then facilitate a discussion about what students think is happening and why. At the end of the week, the caption is published along with information about the event in the photo and other materials. Examining, analyzing, and discussing the stories told in photographs is an engaging way to build students' critical thinking, visual literacy, and language skills. Students who struggle with reading may excel at viewing, giving them the opportunity to be successful and shine in front of their peers.

More for You

Digital Image Collections

- nytimes.com/column/learning-whats-going-on-in-this-picture
- loc.gov/pictures
- artsandculture.google.com
- tessa.lapl.org/photocol

Make It Real

Grades PK–1

- Use images with appropriate content and complexity that are connected to a topic being studied. For example, before a unit on farming, present a picture of a farmer operating a combine.

- Ask students to make observations about what they see in the picture and record these on a chart. Then invite students to share what they think is happening in the picture and give reasons for their thinking.

Grades 2–5

- Have students work in small groups. Give each group a different picture and have them decide what's going on. Then have the groups share their pictures with the class, explaining what they think is going on and why.

- Select images with appropriate content and complexity for your students. The *New York Times* pictures may be appropriate for older students in this grade range.

Grades 6–12

- Layer in additional strategies. For example, you could have students do background research on the topic, write a notebook response about what surprised them, or take turns facilitating class discussions about the pictures.

- Guide students as needed toward making logical inferences rather than competing against one another to get the "right" answer.

Keep in Mind

- This is an excellent opportunity to model how to think about a visual text. For example, *This makes me think about . . . This reminds me of . . . I wonder why . . .*

- A searchable archive of all the photographs presented by the New York Times Learning Network is available, allowing teachers to select pictures that connect to topics or concepts being studied in class.

Book, Head, Heart

Book, Head, Heart (BHH) is a strategy for thinking about text in a meaningful way beyond a simple summary (Beers and Probst 2017). Students first select a passage from a book or text to work with. Next, they summarize what is happening at that point in the text, or they summarize what is going on in their heads while they read. Then they reflect on what is going on in their hearts—how they are feeling about or their emotional reaction to that part of the text.

Make It Real

Grades PK–1	Grades 2–5	Grades 6–12
• Read-aloud or circle time is a great time to practice this strategy and to also build community. • Facilitate the discussion and invite students to talk about the text in terms of their heads and their hearts.	• Use BHH as a think-aloud technique when reading aloud to the whole class. Share your head or heart moments, and then invite students to share. • Create a chart that includes a passage from the text and invite students to add their head or heart moments in words or pictures.	• BHH works well for both independent reading and texts being used for whole-class instruction. • BHH is effective for helping students talk about complex texts in manageable chunks and can be used to spark discussion or give students focus during instructional reading.

Keep in Mind

• Avoid turning this strategy into an activity sheet. The purpose is to guide students to think about a text in a way that is meaningful to them, not to attach extra work to a reading log or homework assignment.

• Have students use BHH to annotate texts. They put a head or a heart to indicate that they are thinking about or feeling a reaction to the passage, and then use that for discussion, questions for the teacher, or a writing response.

Circle Discussion

There are a variety of protocols for engaging students in discussions. Effective discussions take practice, but the benefits are powerful; students' academic vocabulary, discourse skills, and ability to hear other perspectives grow as they think more deeply about texts. Having students sit in a literal circle helps set the stage for creating community during a discussion, and also allows students to see one another. As students develop, they can engage in longer discussions and practice being leaders or facilitators, growing toward more independence from teacher-led discussions.

Make It Real

Grades PK–1

- Hold discussions in teacher-led small groups to support all students in being able to contribute and to sustain their engagement.

- Teach students the Think-Pair-Share protocol. Ask a question and have pairs share their responses with one another. Then have students share with the group.

- Keep large-group discussions short and explicitly teach students the skill of taking turns.

Grades 2–12

Display and teach students talk moves (questions and sentence starters) to use during discussions:

- Can you say more about that?
- What's another way to say that?
- Can you give an example?
- What is your evidence?
- I agree with . . .
- I respectfully disagree . . .
- I would like to add on . . .
- I want to say more about . . .
- That's true because . . .

Keep in Mind

- Students need to be taught specific strategies for engaging in discussions. Do not assume that because they love to talk, they can automatically transition to talking about a concept or text in class.

- Older students can be introduced to more formal discussion protocols such as Fishbowl discussions and Socratic discussions (see Appendix D).

- An important goal for older students is to help grow their independence and level of comfort in engaging in academic discourse. When I am working with a student with high levels of social anxiety, they start by having their discussions one on one with me, they grow to include another support teacher, and then end the year including a few trusted students in their circle.

Focus on Fluency

Reading fluency is the ability to read with accuracy, automaticity, and expression (Rasinski and Young 2024). It is an essential component of reading development. Fluent readers are able to focus on the meaning of what they are reading rather than concentrating on sounding out words. They also have brain space to think metacognitively about a text as they read it. Without fluency, reading comprehension suffers. Students with weak fluency skills read more slowly and often become frustrated because of how long it takes them to read texts. In this section, you'll find engaging strategies for reading fluency practice, including several that incorporate audio or video.

The Strategies

Reader's Theater

Reader's theater is a powerful and effective strategy for building students' reading fluency. Students practice orally reading a text such as a script, speech, or poem in preparation to perform for an audience. Students don't need to memorize their parts. Reader's theater supports and grows fluency because the repeated practice helps students read with expression and builds reading confidence. The best part of reader's theater is that students are typically engaged and motivated by the process (Rasinski and Young 2024).

More for You

Dr. Chase Young's site offers many scripts: thebestclass.org/rtscripts.html

Make It Real

Grades PK–1	Grades 2–5	Grades 6–12
• Work with students as a whole class to practice and perform texts. • Create simple scripts with few words or a combination of words and rebus-style pictures. • Nursery rhymes and chants can be used—write them on chart paper for students to read.	• Choose a read-aloud book to use for reader's theater. • Use or develop scripts that connect to content learning to make the most of instructional time. Social studies content is an excellent source of reader's theater material. • Pair struggling readers with buddies for practice.	• Plays are often included in the secondary curriculum and can be used. Choose several short sections of a play and assign them to different groups of students. • Provide time for students to practice reading the scripts expressively to convey meaning.

Keep in Mind

- Before spending time turning a text into a script, check to see if one already exists. You'll be surprised at what's out there! At the elementary level, literacy texts often come with reader's theater scripts. Just be sure to check copyright information if you are planning a public performance.

- Provide coaching for students to help them develop expressiveness as they read.

- For students who need a challenge, task them with writing the script.

Record Yourself

Have students record themselves reading a text selection. The purpose is for them to prepare their best reading for the recording, which means they will need to practice the reading several times before making a recording. Younger students can simply practice reading and then record themselves. Older students can record themselves, self-assess using a rubric, and then record a revision. This strategy is especially accessible for students who are self-conscious about reading in front of other students.

Make It Real

Grades PK–1

- Support students as they practice before recording. Model fluent reading, and coach them to pay attention to punctuation and read with expression.

- Prereaders can record themselves "reading" nursery rhymes or wordless picture books. This supports learning to read with expression.

- Learning platforms such as SeeSaw allow students to record or take video of themselves and include functions that kids can use to send their recordings to their parents.

Grades 2–5

- This strategy works well during independent work time.

- Have students work on their own or in pairs to practice and then record themselves.

- Students can bring the recordings to a reading conference or small groups for feedback, and then rerecord with revision.

- As an alternative, students can also practice reading to stuffed animals.

Grades 6–12

- Nearly every teenager has a recording device that they carry around in their pockets—a phone! Have them use their phones for practice.

- Students record themselves reading and then self-assess using a fluency rubric. They then rerecord and reflect in writing or during a conference on what they improved with the second reading.

- If students are comfortable, pair them with buddies and have them assess each other using a rubric, give feedback, and then rerecord.

Keep in Mind

- Student recordings can be used to gather data for conferences and reading groups without having to listen to every student read during class.

- Model fluent reading to your students, and discuss how you influence meaning when you speed up, slow down, change the volume of your voice, take pauses, and so on as you read.

- Coaching supports students in becoming fluent readers. Many students need coaching in reading with expression, or *prosody*. Prosody includes volume, pacing, tone, pitch, and phrasing.

Repeated Reading Practice

An important part of developing reading fluency is practice. While there is no one best way to improve fluency skills, repeated reading gives students opportunities to practice word automaticity while layering in prosodic or expressive reading skills. Students need opportunities to verbally manipulate and play with language to become more fluent readers. According to Tim Rasinski and Chase Young, repeated reading helps students "get to deeper levels of expression and meaning" (2024, 9).

More for You

This is an excellent opportunity to work across disciplines. Choose a challenging speech related to the social studies or history curriculum.

Make It Real

Grades PK–1	Grades 2–5	Grades 6–12
• Singing songs, nursery rhymes, and tongue twisters all work to build fluency. At this age, fluency practice should be fun and tap into children's natural desire to play with words, sounds, and rhythm. • Ask students to read the lines to a rhyme such as "One, Two, Buckle My Shoe" in different ways—sadly, happily, and so on. This allows students to play with language.	• Have students use passages from books they're already familiar with—read-alouds, instructional reading books, independent reading books. This supports focusing on fluent reading that shows their comprehension. • Put reading challenge options (see below) on task cards so that students can work with partners and be more independent.	• Choose a text that is initially challenging for students. It can be a bit above their reading level if you read it together first. • Pair students to practice together. Have students read their selections to a small group or the class after they have perfected their reading.

Keep in Mind

Try these reading challenge ideas:

• Read the text at different speeds—what sounds most like normal talking?

• Read in a silly voice.

• Try different phrasing to see what works best.

Poetry Recitation

Call me old school, but memorizing and performing a poem is a fantastic way for students to practice their fluency skills and gain confidence in public speaking. Gone are the days of forcing students to simply memorize poems with a focus on reciting them perfectly, and in are the days of embracing recitation as a way for students to express themselves through the language of poetry. Teachers can frame poetry recitation as an empowering, dynamic, and unique way to play with the nuances of language and infuse meaning and implied tone into their recitations.

Make It Real

Grades PK–1

- Teach students to recite simple poems together. Rhymes, jingles, and songs also work well.

- Practicing songs for a performance or singing songs during circle time both count as poetry recitation.

- Make it fun, make it silly, make it lighthearted, and they'll be hooked!

Grades 2–5

- Challenge students to memorize or read short poems. Poems with rhyme patterns and repetition are easiest for these students to learn.

- Give groups of students one stanza each and practice with them in small groups to create a round robin recitation.

Grades 6–12

- Poetry recitation is growing in popularity thanks to slam poetry competitions and contests like Poetry Out Loud.

- Collaborate with other teachers to hold a poetry competition in your school. Find lesson plans and resources at poetryoutloud.org.

Keep in Mind

A poetry recitation does not have to use a long passage—students can use just one stanza. Remember that the purpose is to practice reading and performing with accuracy and expression—this can still happen with a short passage.

Audio Assistance

Use audio versions of books to help students develop fluent reading skills. Students listen while reading independently, whisper reading, or reading out loud along with the audio. There are many resources available that provide audio versions of stories. Audiobooks support fluency skills by modeling fluent reading and providing an opportunity for students to practice by reading aloud with the audio.

More for You

Many schools subscribe to digital libraries with audiobooks. Additional sources of audio recordings include Storyline Online, PBS KIDS Read-Alongs, Epic!, and Sora.

Make It Real

Grades PK–1	Grades 2–5	Grades 6–12
• Audiobooks are an excellent tool to give students independence in reading books on their own. • Provide a listening station with iPads or tablets so that students can access audio texts using online audio libraries. • Have the physical book available for students to read along with the audio.	• Use audio versions of books to support and supplement instructional reading groups. • Have students listen to books that are at their independent reading levels. Students point to each word in the book as it is read. Next, students try to read aloud along with the recording. They repeat the process until they are able to read the book without the support of the recording.	• Using audio recordings gives older students access to challenging texts that they can't read independently. • Often at these levels, a common text is used to meet learning objectives and provide a shared experience. Providing audio versions allows all students access to that content.

Keep in Mind

- Invite older students to practice reading by creating audio recordings for younger students. They'll be practicing their own fluency as they read. Make the recordings available in the school's online learning platform.

- Technology can be distracting for students. They might have their headphones plugged in but be listening to something else. Make sure students have a clear goal and purpose for their listening work.

Casual Opportunities

Beyond commonly used teaching practices such as direct and explicit instruction, there are many powerful moves that teachers can use to motivate learners and increase students' exposure to literacy skills and concepts. Sometimes the most powerful moments in the classroom are when students use their literacy skills in surprising or unexpected ways.

The Strategies

Word Games

Playing word games with students doesn't have to be complicated, take the place of instructional time, or involve a lot of teacher preparation. Did a lesson end earlier than expected? Is your class a little energetic before lunch and in need of something fun but purposeful? Then play a word game with them. You don't need to plan it and it doesn't need much prep! Word games may not connect with specific texts, but they can be a great way to reinforce word recognition, word study, spelling, and overall vocabulary exposure. Playing these simple and quick games is engaging for all students.

Make It Real

Grades PK–1	Grades 2–5	Grades 6–12
<ul><li>Play "I Spy" to find a letter, vowel team, and so on.</li><li>Play "I Say, You Say." The teacher says a word, the students say the letter it starts with. Or the teacher says a word and students say an opposite word.</li><li>Challenge kids to find as many objects as possible that start with a particular letter.</li></ul>	Popular word games for these levels:<ul><li>"Cast a Spell": The class provides a word and a student with a magic wand spells the word in the air.</li><li>Word ladders</li><li>Scrabble Jr.</li><li>Bananagrams</li><li>Appletters</li><li>Hangman</li></ul>	Students at these levels can play more independently. Keep in mind that they may come up with some interesting words. Think body parts, bodily functions, and so on. Within reason, allow students the opportunity to have fun and play with words.<ul><li>Hink pinks</li><li>Scrabble</li><li>Scattergories</li><li>Quordle</li></ul>

Keep in Mind

There's no need to grade students for this word-game work! The goal is for them to play with words and engage with literacy. You don't need to grade everything, I promise.

Escape Rooms

Escape rooms are an engaging way for students to practice and use both interpersonal and academic skills. They analyze clues, solve puzzles, and think on their feet while they're using analytical, communication, fine-motor, leadership, and social skills. Escape rooms are, of course, fun, but it's important to make sure that there is an educational purpose. When planning, ask yourself, "What is it that students need to learn or gain from doing this?"

More for You

For clues, use puzzles such as riddles, scrambled words, mazes, jigsaw puzzles, codes, and so on.

Make It Real

Grades PK–1

Capture the fun of escape rooms with challenges such as these:

- Send students on a scavenger hunt with clues that lead to a common goal. For example, hide a paper gingerbread man, read *The Gingerbread Man*, then send students on a scavenger hunt to find him.

- Before entering the classroom, give students a task list with items to find that start with a certain letter or sound, or have a certain rhyme pattern. They will feel very important if you give them clipboards!

Grades 2–5

Students this age will need the teacher's oversight and guidance.

- Use the class read-aloud as the jumping off point for escape room challenges.

- Start the challenge with a story that has a problem that needs to be solved. For example, students could solve clues to help Charlotte save Fern in *Charlotte's Web*.

- Develop five tasks for students to solve. Adjust the tasks for students' reading levels.

- Create clues using puzzles to practice and reinforce vocabulary skills and reading skills.

Grades 6–12

Students this age can tackle more complex escape challenges. They can also do digital escape rooms or escapes that require special lock boxes or codes.

- Create escape rooms that require significant close reading and text analysis so students are applying the skills they learn in their ELA class.

- Use an escape room to introduce a concept or topic, or use it at the end of a unit for students to apply what they learned.

Keep in Mind

Free resources for creating escape rooms can be found online and can be a time-saver. If you plan to use premade escape room materials, be sure to vet them for unbiased, grade-level-appropriate content that focuses on learning objectives.

Digital Shorts

Digital Shorts are highly engaging digital stories (often animated) that tend to be no more than ten minutes long. They can be used to reinforce themes, story structure, character development, or content knowledge. For students who are reluctant to engage with reading, they can serve as an on-ramp to the big ideas being explored in shared class texts. There are a multitude of Digital Shorts found easily on YouTube (search "digital shorts for children").

Make It Real

Grades PK–1

Use a Digital Short to spark discussion, offer exposure, or talk about big ideas such as empathy. Connect the Digital Short to a shared read-aloud or to texts being read in instructional reading groups.

Examples:

"La Luna"—"What is a chore that you do for your family that you don't like? How do you feel about it?"

"Lava"—"How do we show people that we love them?"

Grades 2–5

Use Digital Shorts to reinforce story structure:

- Who are the main characters?
- What is the conflict?
- What is the message?
- Sequence the events in the story.

Examples:

"Snack Attack"—"Describe a time you were misunderstood. How did you feel?"

"Hair Love"—"What is something your parents do for you that shows that they love you?"

Grades 6–12

Use Digital Shorts to introduce or reinforce a complex theme and support access to complex ideas for all learners.

Examples:

"The Present"—"How does the twist at the end change our understanding of the character?"

"Loop"—"How can our understanding of others' differences help us to grow compassion?"

"Bao"— "How does grief make people act in unexpected ways?"

Keep in Mind

- Students who struggle with reading can show proficiency in articulating character development, story structure, or theme using Digital Shorts. Digital Shorts can also be used to support literacy learning for EL students or those with reading disabilities.

- Some favorite video shorts, available on YouTube are: "La Luna" (Pixar Short Films #25), "Lava" (DisneyMusicVEVO), "Snack Attack" (Eduardo Verastegui), "Hair Love" (Sony Pictures Animation), "The Present" (Filmakademie Baden-Württemberg), "Loop" (Pixar Sparkshort), and "Bao" (Disney Pixar).

Nature Journaling

Nature journals serve as an avenue for students to capture their observations on paper and then move on to inquiry and deeper thinking about content. Journals reinforce literacy skills by allowing students to process observations, experiences, and content learning through drawing and writing about things they find interesting. Nature journaling is about the power of observation, not about a perfectly crafted written piece, so nature journals support students who have widely varying literacy skills.

Make It Real

Grades PK–1	Grades 2–5	Grades 6–12
• Use a read-aloud about nature as a touchstone text for outside exploration and nature journals. Read the story first, and then use it to guide inquiry. • Provide students with blank paper on clipboards to take outside. Have students draw pictures of what they see and hear. Depending on their level, they can label their pictures or write one or more sentences about their drawings. • Back in the classroom, encourage students to share stories about what they experienced outdoors. Support them in writing more about their drawings.	Have students choose an object in nature and use an "I notice, I wonder" protocol: • Students observe what they notice about the object and draw it in detail. They write about it using descriptive language that details colors, shapes, patterns, and so on. • Students then record wonderings (or questions) about what they are observing. • After returning to the classroom, have students complete research to find out more about what they drew and add that information to their journals.	Have students respond to these prompts: • Take a few photos of ordinary things that you see in a new way (e.g., a cloud that looks like a dragon). • Write down everything you see (people, places, things), hear, physically feel (e.g., the wind on your arms), and emotionally feel (e.g., a sense of calm). • Think about a message you want to convey about your experience. Craft four sentences that capture the message and your sensory description. Pair the writing with your images and add them to a shared (class) slide deck.

Keep in Mind

- Nature journals integrate well with science and math. Students can practice observing, predicting, counting, sorting, and asking questions based on different prompts.

- One of the best lessons I taught was when I spontaneously took my students outside to do some nature journaling. They were reluctant at first but within half an hour they had produced some of their most creative writing of the year.

Letter Writing

In today's world, many students have little experience with sending and receiving actual physical letters. I have found that letter writing is motivating and engaging—not only for writers, but also for the recipients of letters. Letter writing helps students think about an audience other than themselves and supports the development of language and communication skills. There are many possibilities for including letter writing as part of your literacy instruction.

More for You

The Smithsonian National Postal Museum website (postalmuseum.si.edu/for-educators) offers classroom resources and curriculum guides for a range of grade levels and interdisciplinary topics.

Make It Real

Grades PK–1	Grades 2–5	Grades 6–12
• Have students write thank-you letters to special guests who visited your classroom or to people they met during a field trip. Encourage students to give examples of what they liked during the visit. Students can write their own letters, or the class can compose a group letter. • Invite a mail carrier to come to the classroom or arrange a visit to a nearby post office. • Arrange for your students to be pen pals with another class. The class can be at your school or across the world. Engage in shared writing to compose class letters to send back and forth.	Have students write letters to adults in your school community. Pair each student with a former teacher, counselor, or coach: • Give every student a notebook. • Students write a letter in their notebook every week, two weeks, or month, and then deliver it to their buddy. • The buddy responds and then returns the notebook. • Students will love the "delivery": aspect of their notebooks—both delivering and receiving.	• Have students write letters to important people in their lives—a former teacher, coach, counselor, or other person—to express gratitude and let the person know how they are doing. Then mail the letters—this is meaningful for everyone involved. • Have students write to their future selves. Collect and save the letters to mail on an agreed-upon date. • Teach the art of writing email: how to write one, how to respond, how to ask a question or inquire for information, how to write to someone you don't know. This is a life skill that students need to learn.

Letter Writing (cont.)

Keep in Mind

Be sure to include direct instruction about the mechanics of writing a letter: how to address an envelope, where to put a stamp, where to put the address, and how to fold the letter and put it into the envelope. Don't assume students know how to mail a letter!

Recommended Books about Letter Writing

Grades PK–1

- *I Wrote You a Note* by Lizi Boyd
- *Dear Panda* by Miriam Latimer
- *Abuela's Special Letters* (Sofia Martinez series) by Jaqueline Jules

Grades 2–5

- *Same Sun Here* by Silas House and Neela Vaswani
- *I Will Always Write Back* by Caitlin Alifrenka and Martin Ganda
- *The Milk of Birds* by Sylvia Whitman

Grades 6–12

- *We Just Want to Live Here* by Amal Rifa'i and Odella Ainbinder
- *Reading with Patrick* by Michelle Kuo

Making Use of Media

No longer is the use of media limited to displaying physical pictures and occasionally watching an educational program on the one television shared by the department or the entire school. In today's classrooms, a wide range of media can be instantly displayed for all students to see. Media is engaging and offers students rich experiences using visual, auditory, and kinesthetic inputs. Incorporating media into literacy instruction serves several purposes—building background knowledge, strengthening critical thinking, connecting to past and present, and supporting comprehension skills.

The Strategies

Video

Video is a powerful tool to grow background knowledge for all students. Videos create context, help students visualize content, and allow all students access to that content. Videos can level the playing field for students with different learning needs by ensuring that all students can both visualize and understand a concept before beginning to read a text about it. Using videos also increases engagement and interest in the content students are learning.

More for You

Turn on closed captioning to reinforce language skills.

Make It Real

Grades PK–1	Grades 2–5	Grades 6–12
Use shows such as the ones listed to support social-emotional learning and language development: • *Daniel Tiger's Neighborhood* • *Bluey* • *Mr. Rogers' Neighborhood* Videos from these websites support content learning: • BrainPOP Jr. • Mystery Science • Scholastic	When reading informational texts or in-depth fiction, frontload content using videos. The following websites provide a broad range of videos for these levels: • BrainPOP • Mystery Science • Storyline Online • GoNoodle • PBS KIDS • Story Time from Space • Art for Kids Hub • Scholastic	• Before reading a new text, whether fiction or nonfiction, prepare students by showing a short video about the topic and then guide students in understanding key ideas related to the text. • If you are planning on showing a film along with a book, show the film first before reading the book. This will give students a strong foundation of the story and a sense of ownership and engagement as they read.

Keep in Mind

Provide students with goals for watching videos, e.g., *As you watch this video, listen for two facts about the Underground Railroad.*

Realia

When students can see and manipulate real materials, they make strong connections that support recall and comprehension. *Realia* refers to real-life objects that students can handle and experience using their senses. Using realia supports vocabulary development and content knowledge across the curriculum. One of my colleagues took her high school students into the cafeteria's industrial freezer so that they could experience cold like the character in their novel. She took the use of realia to the next level as she sought to connect her students to what they were reading.

Make It Real

Grades PK–1	Grades 2–5	Grades 6–12
Use as many tactile experiences as possible to grow young learners' background knowledge.	Create opportunities for students to use realia to experiment with what they are learning.	Having objects available to manipulate and pass around can scaffold learning and help provide context without seeming too babyish.

Grades PK–1

Examples:

- Read *This Is the Sunflower* by Lola M. Schaefer and then have students dissect a sunflower plant.
- Read *Up in the Garden and Down in the Dirt* by Kate Messner and then grow a small vegetable garden in the spring. Incorporate the food students grow into snack time.
- Read *The Artist* by Ed Vere and have students create their own art to share with the world.

Grades 2–5

Examples:

- Read *Volcanoes!* by Anne Schreiber and build a volcano in the classroom.
- Read *Rise to the Sky* by Rebecca Hirsch and then take students outside to explore and collect artifacts that show the life cycle of a tree.
- Read *Solar Story* by Allan Drummond and build a solar cooker to make s'mores.

Grades 6–12

Examples:

- When reading *Romeo and Juliet*, provide wooden swords and old formal dresses.
- When reading *A Raisin in the Sun*, bring a plant to class and water it every day before class starts.
- When reading *Of Mice and Men*, bring in and pass around hay for students to touch.

Keep in Mind

EL students in particular benefit from realia that connects to what they are learning about. They are learning concrete vocabulary and concepts as well as nuances of language. For example, if you are reading about baseball and have a baseball and bat to pass around, students will be better able to connect the word with the object.

Images, Infographics, Charts, and More

Visual texts such as images and infographics are powerful tools for capturing students' attention and activating and building their background knowledge. Use visuals before reading texts to build vocabulary and increase students' comprehension. Visuals are also useful for presenting key concepts and stimulating thinking and discussion about topics.

More for You

Sources of Infographics and Images

- statista.com
- kidsdiscover.com/infographics
- jpl.nasa.gov/infographics
- nationalgeographic.com/photography
- piktochart.com

Make It Real

Grades PK–1

- Label pictures together to introduce vocabulary around a topic.
- Help students grow their descriptive vocabulary. As you look at pictures together, ask them to use adjectives to describe what they see.
- While reading a story, have students draw what they see. This allows them to focus on the ideas.
- Read a story together, then give students pictures from the book and have them sequence them in order.

Grades 2–5

- Display an interesting image that relates to the text to be read. Have students look at it for a minute. Then ask, "What's going on in this picture?" Ask additional questions until students have shared as much as they can about the picture. Summarize and make connections to the text.
- After reading a text, display a few pictures and have students choose one that best matches the content and explain why.
- Play Pictionary with vocabulary words from a shared text.

Grades 6–12

- Display infographics and charts like those found at statista.com. Have students share their understanding of an infographic and ask questions about what they don't understand. Conduct a think-aloud to help students make sense of the information.
- Have students create their own infographics comparing and contrasting two characters or making a time line of events in a text.
- Use cartoons to teach about sarcasm, word choice, and implied meaning.

Keep in Mind

You can use a website like piktochart.com to develop your own infographics about key concepts you want students to focus on as they read a text. You can make infographics about literary genres, literary terms, and so on.

Gaming

Gaming in the classroom has grown in popularity in recent years, particularly as research has shown positive benefits for students (Franceschini et al. 2013; Fuster-Guilló et al. 2019; Plass, Homer, and Kinzer 2015). Games can increase participation, support social and emotional learning, and even motivate students to take risks. Games require students to manipulate language and make quick decisions—which are skills students use as readers. Games also reinforce comprehension of texts by requiring students to understand what they read and then apply it to game-based situations.

Make It Real

Grades PK–1	Grades 2–5	Grades 6–12
• Scavenger Hunts: Students search for items (or pictures) that start with a target letter (e.g., t—teacher, table, tray) or objects that belong in the same word family (e.g., cat, hat, bat, mat). • Word Searches: Students find words in texts or in the classroom that start with the target letter. • Create Sight Word Bingo cards or Memory game cards with targeted words.	Many gaming sites offer free subscription options you can use to create content for students. In some cases, you can use pre-created content from the site's database. Recommended sites: • Kahoot! • Blooket • Quizizz • SpellingCity • Freerice • Starfall	Students can both play and create games to showcase comprehension. For example, while reading *Romeo and Juliet*, students can create a Kahoot! or GimKit that shows their comprehension. Recommended sites (in addition to the ones suggested for Grades 2–5): • Minecraft Education • Baamboozle • GimKit • Breakout EDU

Keep in Mind

Gaming in the classroom is a fun and engaging way for students to connect to their reading and other content, however, the use of games needs to be deliberate and tied to specific skills or concepts to ensure it has educational benefits.

Primary Sources

Primary sources are documents that give a firsthand view of an event. Examples of primary sources include artifacts, letters, photographs, diary entries, newspapers, and political cartoons. Using primary sources in the classroom connects students to people and events of the past and from other parts of the world. Analyzing primary sources inspires students' curiosity and develops their critical-thinking skills. Primary source materials can be found in many different places—individual homes, government buildings, archives, museums, and so on.

Make It Real

Grades PK–1

- Show students a photograph of a school from the past or from another country and culture. Ask students to describe what they see in the picture and tell how it is like or different from their school.

- Read a text with an account of a school in the past such as *My Great-Aunt Arizona* by Gloria Houston. Discuss how schools in the past were the same as and different from present-day schools.

Grades 2–5

- Identify an informational text students will read and a primary source document that connects to the topic of the text. For example, a text about the civil rights movement and a related poster.

- After reading the text, share the primary source document, and analyze it together. Discuss the message of the document and how it connects to the text.

Grades 6–12

- Select an audio recording of a historical interview, speech, or news report.

- Play the recording (or a portion of it) for the class and provide students with copies of its text. Discuss the theme of the recording and its purpose.

- Have students work in groups to analyze the recording based on its place in history, use of persuasive or argumentative language, any evident bias, and so on, and share their observations.

Keep in Mind

- The Library of Congress website provides digital access to primary source sets for educators (loc.gov/classroom-materials/).

- State and local education departments, archives, and libraries often provide digital access to primary sources related to the history of their service areas.

Inspiration and Imagination

Sometimes the best way to engage our students with content doesn't seem to fit into any one traditional instructional bucket. I have found that when I'm struggling to connect with my students, if I step away from what makes me comfortable in the classroom (a well-structured lesson, for example), we tend to find our way back to each other. This might mean going outside, it might mean using a picture book with older students, or it might mean drinking tea in the persona of a favorite character. The point is that our time and work with students does not need to always be structured within the four walls of the classroom or able to be distilled into a multiple-choice question. Sometimes our work needs to be the exact opposite. The following strategies will help you find tangible, fun, and purposeful ways to do just that.

The Strategies

Take It Outside

No matter what their age, anytime students can get outside, they are excited and engaged. In fact, a growing body of research suggests that the simple act of being outside can have many benefits for young people (Lockwood 2020). Although combining books with being outdoors may seem counterintuitive, it is a great way to motivate and support literacy learning.

Make It Real

Grades PK–1	Grades 2–5	Grades 6–12
• Use sidewalk chalk to play sight-word hopscotch. • Plan an outdoor reading session. Provide snacks and offer books and magazines about the outdoors. • Look for opportunities to match outdoor activities to books, such as having students look for ants outside after reading *Hey, Little Ant* by Phillip and Hannah Hoose.	• Take a nature walk halfway through or after reading aloud a story about the outdoors. • Have book clubs meet outside. Generate excitement by telling students in advance and letting them bring hats and sunglasses. • Allow students to build forts or create special outdoor reading spaces with buddies, and then read in those spaces.	• Let every student write a favorite line from a poem or story in chalk on the sidewalk. • Have independent reading time outside. • Have students choose inspirational quotes from a shared text, make signs, and then put the signs up around the school, neighborhood, or community.

Keep in Mind

- Reading about and observing clouds is accessible and engaging for students of all ages. You'll find lesson plans and resources for different grade levels at the Cloud Appreciation Society website (cloudappreciationsociety.org).

- Being outdoors does not have to mean nature walks in the woods. Going outside could simply mean being on the playground or walking around the block.

Nature as Inspiration

It's amazing what being outdoors and in fresh air can do for students and their vocabulary. Going outdoors is motivating and gives students rich multisensory opportunities for developing vocabulary. However, you don't have to have an entire nature preserve outside to make something real for your students. You can use images and videos online to develop students' vocabulary and give them meaningful experiences related to what they are reading.

Make It Real

Grades PK–1

- Collect items from nature (leaves, sticks, grass, etc.). Ask students to describe them using adjectives only (round, green, crunchy, pokey). Then ask students to give you an adjective and you find an item to match.

- Make an ABC book of items from nature. Take pictures of items during a nature walk and/or have students look for items at home and take pictures of them. Combine the images with text to create a digital book.

Recommended books:

- *Because of an Acorn* by Lola M. Schaefer and Adam Schaefer
- *Owl Moon* by Jane Yolen
- *Henry Hikes to Fitchburg* by D. B. Johnson

Grades 2–5

- Go for a walk as a class and ask each student to bring back one item that has a story. Brainstorm about the items: "I wonder how this item got here?" Introduce terms like *cause and effect*—what caused the leaf to fall from the tree?

- Introduce big ideas about nature—is it our responsibility to care for our planet? In what ways can I learn about other parts of the planet even if I can't go there?

Recommended books:

- *Dr. Art's Guide to Planet Earth for Earthlings* by Art Sussman
- *Flush* by Carl Hiaasen
- *Wild Wings* by Gill Lewis

Grades 6–12

- Go for a walk as a class and ask each student to find or identify three items that can be used to personify nature. Is the stick pointy like a finger? Did the tree reach out its arms to the sky?

- Create poetry corners. Find four to eight poems about the different seasons or about nature or wildlife. Students rotate to different corners to discuss how nature is represented.

Recommended books:

- *Two Degrees* by Alan Gratz
- *Reading the Forested Landscape* by Tom Wessels
- *A Walk in the Woods* by Bill Bryson

Keep in Mind

- Don't assume that students know how to look at the details of nature—many will need to be taught to observe the features of items gathered during a walk or how to spot treasures to bring back to your learning spaces.

- Display images while reading about a setting or concept so that students can visualize it. For example, if students are reading about the Oregon Trail, show images of the landscape so they can make the connection.

Character Social Hour

During a character social hour, each student assumes the role of a character and then socializes with the class as their character. This allows students to identify their favorite characters; imagine how the characters look, speak, and think; and then share their interpretations of the characters. There are several ways to structure and support students as they do this.

Make It Real

Grades PK–1	Grades 2–5	Grades 6–12
• Have students dress up as their characters. Provide a collection of simple props students can use rather than full costumes. • Have students introduce themselves to the class as their characters and tell the class about themselves. Prompt and coach students to speak as if they were the characters. • Trace students' bodies on big paper and then have them illustrate and decorate the characters they choose.	• Use a common text such as a read-aloud. Before assigning roles, collaborate as a class to map out the characteristics and personalities of the characters in the book. • Give students task cards with the character's name and a checklist of their traits. • The socializing might last only five to ten minutes; then the students come back together and share who they met.	• Have a character social hour as a pre-reading activity. Give students descriptions of characters and have them act accordingly. • Have students introduce themselves as their characters. • Give students questions to ask one another if they get stuck in conversation. • Challenge students to pair up with the character who they think they would connect with the best.

Keep in Mind

- Ask students to imagine what their characters' favorites might be, such as favorite food, favorite vacation, favorite movie, favorite song, and so on.

- Challenge younger students to write postcards to characters they "met" and invite them to do something they both would like.

- As a stretch for older students, have them each assume the persona of a character and then participate in a Socratic discussion (see Appendix E).

Thinking Outside the Box

Using one's imagination doesn't always come easy. Guide students through thinking in different ways with books like *Not a Box* by Antoinette Portis. This story invites children of all ages to think about how ordinary items like a box, a stick, an umbrella, or even a jar can be something more than what they actually are. Could that box be a boat? Could that stick be a sword? Could that umbrella be a shield? Could that jar be a fairy house? Encourage creativity and wondering to help students think about the "what ifs" in this world.

More for You

Antoinette Portis has also written *Not a Stick*.

Make It Real

Grades PK–1

- Read *Not a Box*. Brainstorm together—what else could a box be?

- Bring in other items—a stick, an umbrella, a ball. Ask students to follow the pattern of the text and share their ideas of what the items can be.

- Display the words students generate on a word wall.

Grades 2–5

- After reading *Not a Box*, have students use the following frame to write their own sentences: *This is not a box, it's a _____.*

- Invite students to elaborate and expand their sentences to tell more of a story. For example, *This is not a box, it's an ambulance, zooming through crowded streets.*

Grades 6–12

- After reading *Not a Box*, have students write *This is not a box, it's a _____* on a piece of paper and complete it. Toss the papers into the middle of the classroom and have all students go take one and read it aloud.

- Using *Not a Box* as a common text, teach students about metaphor/extended metaphor and then have them create their own *Not a . . .* stories.

Keep in Mind

- Have students create *Not a . . .* books. Create a class book with younger students. Have students from grade 2 on create their own books to share with others.

- It may be more difficult for older students to harness their imaginations; sometimes anonymity can help get those creative minds started.

- Turn this into a STEAM activity by having students build or create the objects they are imagining.

Goals and Reflection

Goal setting helps students take responsibility for learning and develop growth mindsets. Reflecting on both what they want to learn and what they have learned is motivating and empowering. When you are sailing in the middle of a lake, you often don't realize how far you have come until you look behind you and see the shrinking shoreline. Being a learner in a classroom is a similar experience, which is why teachers should give students opportunities to set goals and then notice the growth they have made along the way.

Make It Real

Grades PK–1

- Create posters with goals. For example, *I can name the letters of the alphabet.* Students write their names on the posters when they reach the goal.

- Create a notebook for each student with pages for each goal. Have students sign the pages when they reach a goal.

- Sample prompts: "What are you proud of learning this week? What is something you are working on learning?"

Grades 2–5

- Encourage students to set their own goals. Provide 4 x 6 cards with sentence frames for students to record their goals, the date they plan to reach them, and the steps they will take.

- Sample goals: My goal is to read _____ chapter books by the end of the month. My goal is to learn _____ new words this week. My goal is to practice reading aloud every day for 10 minutes.

Grades 6–12

- Use circle discussions to give students opportunities to share what they have learned and what goals they have moving forward.

- Sample goals: I will read for 20 minutes every day outside of class. I will use sticky notes to record my thinking while I read so that I don't forget. I will read _____ books this month.

Keep in Mind

- Take time to celebrate students' progress. This can be as a whole class, in reading groups, or individually with the teacher.

- It's important that goals be about the individual student growth and not competition between students. It's okay if one student only reads one book and another reads ten. If the work for both of those students represents growth and perseverance, then they have both been successful.

- Older students can keep reading logs where they record the number of pages in each book. At the end of the quarter, have students divide the total number of pages they read by the number of weeks in the quarter. Their final number is their average weekly reading rate. They can make bar graphs tracking their average weekly reading rates, and then reflect quarterly on their progress.

Conferences and Connection

Reading conferences should be a foundational component of literacy instruction, regardless of the grade level of students. Yet they are sometimes the first thing to go when we are crunched for time or struggling with classroom management. They can be challenging to manage, challenging to provide consistently, and challenging to handle with large classes. However, they are essential as a time to check in with readers and provide individualized feedback and instruction. The following strategies offer several approaches to the reading conference, each serving a different purpose and requiring varying amounts of time and effort. Reading conferences are not meant to replace direct instruction in literacy skills, but rather to support students as they practice those skills and they grow as readers.

The Strategies

1:1 Reading Conferences

The 1:1 reading conference is a means of connecting with students, a way to see how students are applying a particular skill, and a tool for supporting students who are struggling or who need extension and enrichment. These conferences provide information about students' strengths and needs, which you can then use to differentiate instruction. Spend the first minute as an SEL check-in, then prompt students with questions about their reading progress and comprehension.

Make It Real

Grades K–2

- Ask the student about a book they self-selected. Ask why they chose it and what they like about it.

- Have the student read a brief section to you from an instructional text. Try to give them at least one compliment about their reading.

- After the student reads, provide support and coaching to develop phonics, fluency, or another skill.

- Collect data about students' strengths and reading needs and use it to inform instruction.

Grades 3–5

- Have the student read aloud either their instructional text or a self-selected text. Try to give them at least one compliment about their reading.

- Ask the student to summarize what is happening in the text and what they think will happen next. Ask the student to give text evidence that supports any inferences or predictions they make.

- Offer a strategy the student can use to improve reading.

- Collect data about students' strengths and reading needs.

Grades 6–12

- Determine a focus for conferences. For example: The student will read aloud a short passage and explain what they do when they are stuck.

- Aim to meet with two to three students per class period while other students work independently. Try to meet with each student at least once a month.

- Ask the student what they're currently reading, what page they're on, what rating they would give their book and why.

- Spend time discussing the book with the student—the content, what the student thinks about it, and so on.

Keep in Mind

- Keep records of your reading conferences with students. Some teachers keep a binder with a page for each student for capturing this information.

- If you start to see a pattern emerge out of 1:1 reading conferences, plan for direct instruction for the whole class or for flexible, needs-based small groups.

The Daily Check-In

The daily check-in is a quick way to touch base with students about their reading progress. The teacher calls on students and they say what they are reading and how much progress they have made. If students have changed books, this is an opportunity for them to report that. While relatively simple, when done consistently, the daily check-in provides useful long-term insight into students' reading patterns.

Make It Real

Grades 2–5	Grades 6–12
• During independent reading, walk around the room and ask students the title of the book they are reading and the page they are on. Record this information.	• This works well as a daily three- or four-minute routine at the start of class and can double as a way to take attendance.
• Check in with students daily or every two or three days to record whether they are still reading the same book and what page they are now on.	• Each student shares the title of their book and what page they're on. The teacher takes simple notes such as *finished, quit, new book, forgot book*.
• As an alternative, during whole-group time, have students share the title of a book they are reading, talk about a favorite character, or make a prediction about what they think will happen next.	• Avoid judgment as students report on their reading progress (or lack of progress). Compliment students who are making good progress.

Keep in Mind

- Information collected during the daily check-in can be used to inform individual conferences with students.

- The daily check-in is a powerful way to connect with students if you teach multiple classes. The information gathered is often much more than simply a page number. You might learn that a student left a book at a relative's house and won't be able to get it for a few weeks, or that a student has quit three books in a row. This information allows you to determine next steps in supporting students' independent reading.

Roving Conferences

While students are working independently, the teacher moves around the room and pauses to have brief conversations with students. These are relatively quick conferences where the focus is on providing scaffolds for students who need them, offering positive feedback, or pushing student learning a bit further. In addition to offering students timely guidance, circulating among students helps them stay focused on the task at hand.

Make It Real

Grades PK–1	Grades 2–5	Grades 6–12
• Invite students to tell you about a book they are reading or other work they are doing. Ask specific questions such as, "Who are the characters in this story? What are they doing? What do you think is happening in this picture? What happens at the end of the story?" • If students are reading books, let them know you notice reading behaviors they are using such as pointing to each word, carefully looking at the illustrations, and sounding out words.	• After direct instruction, check in with students about the skills or strategies you taught. For example, making inferences or paying attention to punctuation. • If a student is requesting help, let them know you will get to them with comments such these: "I see you need me. I'm making my way around the room." Or, "Don't worry if you feel stuck, try it, and I'll be right over to see how you did."	• After a lesson on a topic such as symbolism, give each student a sticky note and have them use it to flag where they think they notice a symbol. As you circulate, use the sticky notes as conversation starters. • Use statements such as these to support students as you circulate: "I'm going to return in a few minutes and you can show me what you tried." Or, "I see you haven't started; how can I help?"

Keep in Mind

- Consider taking brief notes on your conversations with each student. This will help you remember and notice patterns over time.

- Squat down so you are at a student's eye level. Some teachers carry around a small stool so they can sit next to students. Try to avoid leaning over students.

- If you notice several students who need support on a specific skill, you can pull them together for a focus conference (see page 76) to offer re-instruction.

Focus Conferences

Focus conferences are small, flexible groups formed to provide direct instruction around a particular skill. Often a focus conference group is created based on observations during roving or 1:1 conferences. They work best with four or five students who would benefit from instruction on the same skill. Students could be reading a common text or different books about a common topic. Focus conferences allow for targeted support and instruction for different groups of students. I have sorted students many different ways—by what skill I want to teach, by the book they are reading, by the genre we are studying . . . there are many possibilities.

Make It Real

Grades 2–5	Grades 6–12
• Focus conferences work well to reinforce a specific skill with a small group of students who need it. They can also be used to provide students with additional challenge. • As an alternative to leveled reading groups, students can be grouped for different needs depending on the text or instructional needs.	• Students this age can self-select an area of focus: "Do you want to focus on symbolism or theme today? Do you want to look at vivid imagery or alliteration today? Do you want to track how a character is changing or highlight their flaws?" • Groups with a self-selected focus should be relatively short and, while teacher-directed, allow students to learn from each other.

Keep in Mind

How you create groups for focus conferences will be based on other conferencing work happening in the classroom. You can use data gathered from 1:1 conferences, roving conferences, or daily check-ins to inform these flexible groups.

Peer Conferences

A peer conference is when students meet together to discuss what they are reading. They aren't conferring with one another for purposes of instruction, but rather to have a conversation about books. During the conference, students respond to prompts to discuss the books. The teacher circulates around the room, listening to the conversations and noting areas where students will benefit from additional instruction and support. Students will need modeling and coaching on how to have book discussions and what it means to be productive as a pair.

Make It Real

Grades 3–5	Grades 6–12
• Have students discuss their independent reading books. They can ask one another questions and take notes. • Give students a form to complete that has questions to ask and space for writing the answers. Questions can vary depending on whether students are reading fiction or informational texts. • Provide a specific amount of time for each student to ask questions and record their classmate's responses. Allow 10 to 15 minutes total for both students to take a turn.	• Pair students who are reading the same text. Provide a menu of items that focus specifically on the text and invite collaboration. For example, "Agree on the most important line in your section and highlight it. Identify where the writer is using descriptive language. Find a symbol that you have a hunch might develop into something bigger." • After the conferences, have students self-assess using a rubric. This will give you feedback on their work and what they need next.

Keep in Mind

Creating pairings can be challenging as students get older. They want to be with their friends, but they might be at different reading levels. You can ask students who they'd like to pair with, or you can have them choose their books and then pair them accordingly.

Children's Literature

Alifirenka, Caitlin, and Martin Ganda. 2016. *I Will Always Write Back: How One Letter Changed Two Lives*. New York: Little, Brown Books for Young Readers.

Boyd, Lizi. 2017. *I Wrote You a Note*. San Francisco: Chronicle Books.

Bryson, Bill. 2007. *A Walk in the Woods: Rediscovering America on the Appalachian Trail*. New York: Vintage Books.

Drummond, Allan. 2020. *Solar Story: How One Community Lives Alongside the World's Biggest Solar Plant*. New York: Farrar, Straus and Giroux.

Gratz, Alan. 2022. *Two Degrees*. New York: Scholastic.

Hansberry, Lorraine. 1959. *A Raisin in the Sun*. New York: Random House.

Hatkoff, Isabella, and Craig Hatkoff. 2006. *Owen and Mzee: The True Story of a Remarkable Friendship*. New York: Scholastic.

Hiaasen, Carl. 2010. *Flush*. New York: Random House.

Hirsch, Rebecca E. 2023. *Rise to the Sky: How the World's Tallest Trees Grow Up*. Minneapolis, MN: Lerner.

Hoose, Phillip, and Hannah Hoose. 1998. *Hey, Little Ant*. New York: Random House.

House, Silas, and Neela Vaswani. 2013. *Same Sun Here*. Somerville, MA: Candlewick Press.

Houston, Gloria. 1992. *My Great-Aunt Arizona*. New York: HarperCollins.

Johnson, D. B. 2000. *Henry Hikes to Fitchburg*. New York: HarperCollins.

Jules, Jacqueline. 2017. *Abuela's Special Letters*. Mankato, MN: Capstone.

Kamkwamba, William, and Bryan Mealer. 2016. *The Boy Who Harnessed the Wind, Young Reader's Edition*. New York: Penguin Young Readers.

Keats, Ezra Jack. 1962. *The Snowy Day*. New York: Penguin Young Readers.

Kinney, Jeff. 2007. *Diary of a Wimpy Kid*. New York: Amulet.

Kuo, Michelle. 2017. *Reading with Patrick: A Teacher, a Student, and a Life-Changing Friendship*. New York: Random House.

Latimer, Miriam. 2014. *Dear Panda*. Toronto: Owlkids.

Lee, Harper. 1960. *To Kill a Mockingbird*. New York: HarperCollins.

Lewis, Gill. 2011. *Wild Wings*. New York: Atheneum Books for Young Readers.

McManis, Charlene Willing, with Traci Sorell. 2019. *Indian No More*. New York: Lee and Low.

Messner, Kate. 2015. *Up in the Garden and Down in the Dirt*. San Francisco: Chronicle Books.

Nesbø, Jo. 2009. *Doctor Proctor's Fart Powder*. New York: Aladdin.

Pilkey, Dav. 2013. *The Adventures of Captain Underpants*. New York: Scholastic.

Portis, Antoinette. 2006. *Not a Box*. New York: HarperCollins.

Portis, Antoinette. 2007. *Not a Stick*. New York: HarperCollins.

Rifa'i, Amal, and Odelia Ainbinder. 2003. *We Just Want to Live Here: A Palestinian Teenager, an Israeli Teenager, An Unlikely Friendship*. New York: St. Martin's.

Sachar, Louis. 2000. *Holes*. New York: Random House.

Schaefer, Lola M. 2000. *This Is the Sunflower*. New York: HarperCollins.

Schaefer, Lola M., and Adam Schaefer. 2016. *Because of an Acorn*. San Francisco: Chronicle Books.

Schreiber, Anne. 2008. *Volcanoes!* Glendale, CA: Disney Publishing.

Sendak, Maurice. 1963. *Where the Wild Things Are*. New York: HarperCollins.

Shakespeare, William. 1977. *Romeo and Juliet (Folger Shakespeare Library Series)*. Logan, IA: Perfection Learning.

Steig, William. 1970. *Sylvester and the Magic Pebble*. New York: Simon and Schuster.

Steinbeck, John. 1937. *Of Mice and Men*. New York: Penguin.

Sussman, Art. 2000. *Dr. Art's Guide to Planet Earth: For Earthlings Ages 12 to 120*. Chelsea, VT: Chelsea Green Publishing.

Vere, Ed. 2023. *The Artist*. New York: Random House.

Wessels, Tom. 2005. *Reading the Forested Landscape: A Natural History of New England*. New York: Countryman Press.

White, E. B. 1952. *Charlotte's Web*. New York: HarperCollins.

Whitman, Sylvia. 2014. *The Milk of Birds*. New York: Atheneum Books for Young Readers.

Wilder, Laura Ingalls. 1953. *Little House on the Prairie*. New York: HarperCollins.

Yolen, Jane. 1987. *Owl Moon*. New York: Penguin Young Readers.

References

Adams, John. 1761. *The Adams Papers, Diary and Autobiography of John Adams*, Vol. 1, *1755–1770*, ed. L. H. Butterfield. Cambridge, MA: Harvard University Press, 1961. founders.archives.gov/documents/Adams/01-01-02-0006-0008.

Allington, Richard L., and Anne M. McGill-Franzen. 2021. "Reading Volume and Reading Achievement: A Review of Recent Research." *Reading Research Quarterly* 56 (S1): S231–S238. doi.org/10.1002/rrq.404.

Allred, Johnny B., and Michael E. Cena. 2020. "Reading Motivation in High School: Instructional Shifts in Student Choice and Class Time." *Journal of Adolescent & Adult Literacy* 64 (1): 27–35. doi.org/10.1002/jaal.1058.

Beers, Kylene, and Robert E. Probst. 2017. *Disrupting Thinking: Why How We Read Matters*. New York: Scholastic.

Bogard, Jennifer M., and Lisa Donovan. 2022. *Integrating the Arts in Language Arts: 30 Strategies to Create Dynamic Lessons, Second Edition*. Huntington Beach, CA: Shell Education.

Cantrell, Susan Chambers, Jessica Pennington, Margaret Rintamaa, Monica Osborne, Cindy Parker, and Mary Rudd. 2017. "Supplemental Literacy Instruction in High School: What Students Say Matters for Reading Engagement." *Reading & Writing Quarterly* 33 (1): 54–70.

Duke, Nell K., and Kelly B. Cartwright. 2021. "The Science of Reading Progresses: Communicating Advances Beyond the Simple View of Reading." *Reading Research Quarterly* (Special Issue) 56 (S1): S25–S44. doi.org/10.1002/rrq.411.

Erbeli, Florina, and Marianne Rice. 2021. "Examining the Effects of Silent Independent Reading on Reading Outcomes: A Narrative Synthesis Review from 2000 to 2020." *Reading & Writing Quarterly* 38 (3): 253–271. doi.org/10.1080/10573569.2021.1944830.

Erickson, Karen. 2016. "Connecting Drama with Language Arts." Arts Integration in Education (blog), February 1, 2016. creativedirections.org/arts-integration/connecting-drama-language-arts/.

Franceschini, Sandro, Simone Gori, Milena Ruffino, Simona Viola, Massimo Molteni, and Andrea Facoetti. 2013. "Action Video Games Make Dyslexic Children Read Better." *Current Biology* 23 (6): 462–466. doi.org/10.1016/j.cub.2013.01.044.

Fuster-Guilló, Andrés, María Luisa Pertegal-Felices, Antonio Jimeno-Morenilla, Jorge Azorín-López, María Luisa Rico-Soliveres, and Felipe Restrepo-Calle. 2019. "Evaluating Impact on Motivation and Academic Performance of a Game-Based Learning Experience Using Kahoot." *Frontiers in Psychology* 10 Article 2843: 1–8.

Gallagher, Kelly. 2009. *Readicide: How Schools Are Killing Reading and What You Can Do About It*. Portland, ME: Stenhouse.

Gilson, Cindy M., Kristen D. Beach, and Samantha L. Cleaver. 2018. "Reading Motivation of Adolescent Struggling Readers Receiving General Education Support." *Reading & Writing Quarterly* 34 (6): 505–522. doi.org/10.1080/10573569.2018.1490672.

Hasselbring, Ted S., and Laura I. Goin. 2004. "Literacy Instruction for Older Struggling Readers: What Is the Role of Technology?" *Reading & Writing Quarterly* 20 (2): 123–144. doi.org/10.1080/10573560490262073.

Hollie, Sharroky. n.d.-a. "What We Do." Center for Culturally Responsive Teaching and Learning. Accessed July 25, 2023. culturallyresponsive.org/what-we-do.

Hollie, Sharroky. n.d.-b. "Validate, Affirm, Build and Bridge (VABB™)." Center for Culturally Responsive Teaching and Learning. Accessed July 25, 2023. culturallyresponsive.org/vabb.

Learned, Julie E. 2018. "Classroom Contexts and the Construction of Struggling High School Readers." *Teachers College Record: The Voice of Scholarship in Education* 120 (8): 1–47. doi.org/10.1177/016146811812000802.

Lee, Jung-Sook. 2013. "The Relationship between Student Engagement and Academic Performance: Is It a Myth or Reality?" *The Journal of Educational Research* 107 (3): 177–185. doi.org/10.1080/00220671.2013.807491.

Lockwood, Katie K. 2020. "The Benefits of Outdoor Play: Why It Matters." Health Tip of the Week (blog), July 28, 2020. chop.edu/news/health-tip/benefits-outdoor-play-why-it-matters#.

Neugebauer, Sabina Rak. 2017. "Assessing Situated Reading Motivations across Content Areas: A Dynamic Literacy Motivation Instrument." *Assessment for Effective Intervention* 42 (3): 131–149. doi.org/10.1177/1534508416666067.

Plass, Jan L., Bruce D. Homer, and Charles K. Kinzer. 2015. "Foundations of Game-Based Learning." *Educational Psychologist* 50 (4): 258–283. doi.org/10.1080/00461520.2015.1122533.

Rasinski, Timothy, and Chase Young. 2024. *Build Reading Fluency: Practice and Performance with Reader's Theater and More, Second Edition*. Huntington Beach, CA: Shell Education.

Scarborough, Hollis S. 2001. "Connecting Early Language and Literacy to Later Reading (Dis)abilities: Evidence, Theory, and Practice." In *Handbook of Early Literacy Research*, edited by Susan B. Neuman and David K. Dickinson, 97–110. New York: The Guilford Press.

Scholastic with Fluent. 2022. *Kids and Family Reading Report™, 8th Edition*. scholastic.com/content/corp-home/kids-and-family-reading-report.html.

Shanahan, Timothy. 2018. "Where Questioning Fits Comprehension: Skills and Strategies." Reading Rockets: Shanahan on Literacy (blog), June 1, 2018. readingrockets.org/blogs/English-literacy/where-questioning-fits-comprehension-instruction-skills-and-strategies.

Stanovich, Keith E. 1986. "Matthew Effects in Reading: Some Consequences of Individual Differences in the Acquisition of Literacy." *Reading Research Quarterly* 21 (4): 360–407. doi.org/10.1598/rrq.21.4.1.

Tegmark, Mats, Tarja Alatalo, Monika Vinterek, and Mikael Winberg. 2022. "What Motivates Students to Read at School? Student Views on Reading Practices in Middle and Lower Secondary School." *Journal of Research in Reading* 45 (1): 100–118. doi.org/10.1111/1467-9817.12386.

Tokan, Moses Kopong, and Mbing Maria Imakulata. 2019. "The Effect of Motivation and Learning Behaviour on Student Achievement." *South African Journal of Education* 39 (1). doi.org/10.15700/saje.v39n1a1510.

Wilhelm, Jeffrey. 2013. *Deepening Comprehension with Action Strategies: Role Plays, Text-Structure Tableaux, Talking Statues, and Other Enactment Techniques That Engage Students with Text,* Revised Edition. New York: Scholastic.

Wilhelm, Jeffrey D., and Michael W. Smith. 2016. "The Power of Pleasure Reading: What We Can Learn from the Secret Reading Lives of Teens." *The English Journal* 105 (6): 25–30. jstor.org/stable/26359251.

Name_____ Date_____

Tips for BookSnaps

Directions: Make a BookSnap that shows your thoughts about a text. You will need an app that allows you to take a photo and mark it up.

1. Think about the text as you read it.
   - What connections do you make?
   - How does it make you feel?
   - What lines speak to you?
   - What questions do you have?

2. Take a picture of a passage that you want to share.

3. Use markup tools to underline or highlight lines that speak to you. You can also circle text or use arrows.

4. Create a textbox and share your ideas about the passage.
   - thoughts
   - questions
   - comments
   - themes

5. Add emojis, stickers, hashtags, etc., that show your ideas about the passage.

6. Use a text box to add the title and author of the passage.

7. Share your BookSnap with your classmates!

Name _____ Date _____

My Book Tasting Notes

Directions: Try a "taste" of some new books!

Title: _____ _____ _____ Genre: _____ Three words about the cover: _____ _____ _____ Read a few pages. What do you think? _____ _____ _____ _____ Thumbs up/thumbs down:	Title: _____ _____ _____ Genre: _____ Three words about the cover: _____ _____ _____ Read a few pages. What do you think? _____ _____ _____ _____ Thumbs up/thumbs down:

Name _____ Date _____

Reading Bingo

Directions: Complete these activities. Do four in a row to get BINGO!

Read outside.	Listen to someone read to you.	Read something at home that is not a book.	Record yourself reading.
Use your whisper voice to read.	Read with a friend.	Listen to an audiobook.	Draw your favorite part of a book.
Reread a favorite book.	Read a book about an animal.	Read to a toy or stuffed animal.	Read in bed.
Read a poem.	Read in a comfy spot.	Read under a tree.	Read to a grown-up.

Name _____ Date _____

Reading Bingo

Directions: Complete these activities. Do five in a row to get BINGO!

Read outside.	Listen to someone read to you.	Read something at home that is not a book.	Read a chapter book.	Read before breakfast.
Use your whisper voice to read.	Read a book about nature.	Listen to an audiobook.	Record yourself reading.	Read a book set in a different country.
Read a book about a historical event.	Read with a friend.	Read a book about friendship.	Read in bed.	Read a graphic novel.
Read a poem.	Read in a comfy spot.	Read a book in a series.	Read to someone on the phone or on the computer.	Read a mystery.
Read a nonfiction text.	Read to someone younger than you.	Read under a tree.	Read a fantasy book.	Reread a favorite book.

Discussion Protocols

Fishbowl Discussion

Fishbowl discussion involves a small group of students sitting in a circle engaged in discussion, while students sitting in an outer circle observe and reflect on the process or the content of the discussion. This is good practice for longer discussions that students will need to facilitate, and it supports students who are not comfortable talking with the larger group.

Socratic Discussion

A Socratic discussion is based on the teaching methods of Socrates and is a method of learning through discussion. Students read a common text in advance and create topics or questions for discussion collaboratively. They also prepare evidence to support those topics. When I do this with high schoolers, we watch examples of Socratic discussions, define norms for discussion together, and then practice before the discussion. I prefer to have students prepared enough that I do not participate, but I will provide support if needed. Allowing students the opportunity to guide their own inquiry by teaching them how to ask meaningful questions supports their engagement and thinking about complex issues.

Digital Resources

Accessing the Digital Resources

The digital resources can be downloaded by following these steps:

1. Go to www.tcmpub.com/digital

2. Use the 13-digit ISBN number to redeem the digital resources.

3. Respond to the question using the book.

4. Follow the prompts on the Content Cloud website to sign in or create a new account.

5. The content redeemed will appear on your My Content screen. Click on the product to look through the digital resources. All file resources are available for download. Select files can be previewed, opened, and shared. Any web-based content, such as videos, links, or interactive text, can be viewed and used in the browser but is not available for download.

For questions and assistance with your ISBN redemption, please contact Teacher Created Materials.

email: customerservice@tcmpub.com

phone: 800-858-7339